CLACKAMAS LITERARY REVIEW

2015
Volume XIX

Clackamas Community College
Oregon City, Oregon

CLACKAMAS LITERARY REVIEW

Managing Editor
Trevor Dodge

Associate Editors

Marlene Broemer   Trista Cornelius   Sean Davis

Sue Mach   Jeff McAlpine   Nicole Rosevear

Matthew Warren

Assistant Editors & Designers

Samantha Batey   Donald Beach   Julia Berezhnoy

Janel Brubaker   Vitaliy Burlaka   Angela Douglass

Chelsie Gaither   Leslie Garrick   Elissa Johnson

Vera Johnson   Victoria Marinelli   Delilah Martinez

Shilo Niziolek

Cover Art

Spirals and Rings by Julia Stoops. Collection of Todd Putnam.

The *Clackamas Literary Review* is published annually at Clackamas Community College. Manuscripts are read from September 1st to December 31st and will not be returned. By submitting your work to *CLR*, you indicate your consent for us to publish that work in print and online. This issue is $10; issues I–XI are $6 if ordered through *CLR*; issues XII–XVIII are available through your favorite online bookseller.

Clackamas Literary Review
19600 Molalla Avenue, Oregon City, Oregon 97045
ISBN: 978-0-9796882-7-0
Printed by Lightning Source
www.clackamasliteraryreview.org

CONTENTS

PROSE

POSSIBILITY

Editor's Note

Color. It's a byproduct of light's spectral nature; it's particular to how our eyes receive it, and how our brains process it. The primary way we receive and perceive light is how it is reflected, refracted, or ultimately absorbed by all objects and matter. By using a prism to shatter rays of light into their spectral patterns, we've been able to project our perceptions about our world and our position into the known universe and have them return to us as both certainty and mystery. Because the more we *see*, the more curious and inquisitive we become. The more we *see*, the more we *want to know*. When colors reveal themselves to us, so does the matter being reflected, refracted, absorbed.

CLR. It's a byproduct of art's spectral nature; it, too, is particular to how our eyes receive it, and how our brains process it. The 2015 issue you're holding in your hands in this moment of perception is one we've waited for a very long time to share with you. These are words and images of possibility, refracted through the spectral patterns of joy and despair, of hope and haunt, of knowledge and ignorance. These are words and images not *of* light, but *light itself.*

We want you to feel the weight of light in your hands now. Close the book and your eyes. Go ahead, it's okay. We've been practicing while we were waiting for you. Close the book, close your eyes, and feel what you've already seen. All the light in all of existence traveled through space and time to reach *you*. Why, then, should this be any different?

C[o]*L*[o]*R*. Place your eyes between the consonants. Reflect. Refract. *Absorb.*

A Few Items at this Moment

Robert Wrigley

The sky is cloudless and there is no wind.
Wholly encased in snow, the trees
at the mountaintop are not beyond
words but beyond my willingness

to diminish them, their blue shadows,
the silence. There are a few items
at this moment no one in the world knows
but me, and I choose not to say them,

not even to the mountain or the trees,
to whom they would not matter anyway,
being in all ways, just now, wordless,
having absolutely nothing to say

about a man who's merely come this way
and does not speak and cannot stay.

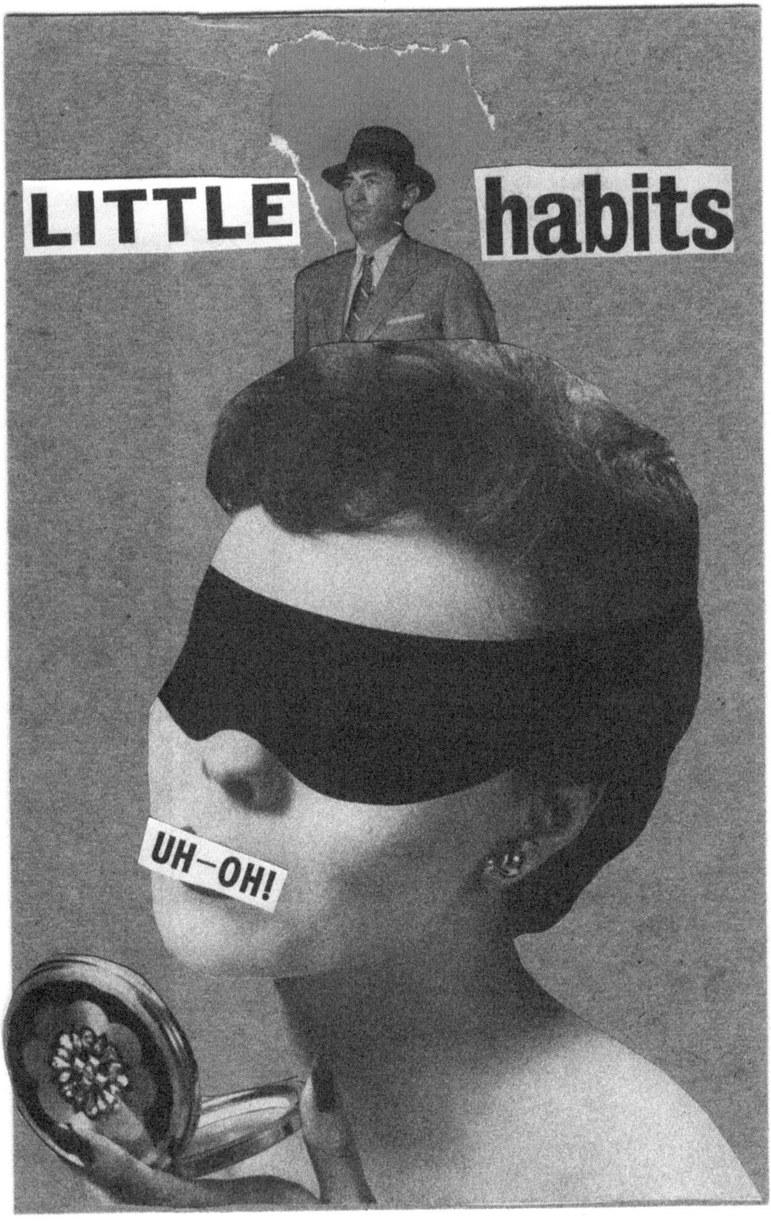
LITTLE
habits
UH-OH!

My Marty

Lois Rosen

That hip, the smell of that skin, the indrawn breath and then the exhale: how beautiful his body was, if you could say that about a man, my Marty, forty-four years old then, smelling of Old Spice and sex, falling so deeply asleep afterwards, the pale cheeks of his backside as solid-looking as that sculpture of Michelangelo's David in *Life* magazine, that David on his road to becoming King of all Israel, and my Marty, the king of my life, *I will fear no evil for thou art with me.*

In our living room, turned into a bedroom each night, I gripped my top sheet to dab my tears. Whatever people said behind our backs about his ruined face, pitying us, how little they knew, any of them. None of them saw him below the neck, did they?

Words flung at me in the hospital's fluorescent glare a dozen years ago still stung. I recalled how that Doctor Samuelson, number one cancer surgeon, white-jacketed, stony-eyed expert, warned me in his haughty voice, "Mrs. Rabinowitz, your husband will most likely live only a few more weeks if he doesn't start eating. You've got to try coaxing him more."

Spoonful by spoonful, rice cereal, pudding, applesauce I ground with a vengeance in the Foley Foodmill, and of course, chicken soup, I tipped gingerly into his mouth. *Live, goddamn you, live.*

And he had, thanks to God, too. But one night after no sex for that dry-dry year of his illness and recovery, his face buried in his pillow, his back to me, maybe he was still half asleep, maybe the exterior wounds had healed enough. I don't know why, not really, but he turned toward me, rested his good cheek on my breasts, and let me cradle his head.

"It's all right," I said. "It's all right."

He raised my nightgown, the lace and his fingertips sliding up my thighs.

So with our Harriet at camp and our Al away for the summer, in our side-by-side pull-out beds from the Castro Convertible sofa, chest hair curled and black on his skin, white as that doctor's immaculate jacket, I placed my palm on the skin above his stomach. My hand rose and fell with his breath, his rhythm relaxing my breath.

Finally, Marty and I could make love as noisily and often as we wanted, not that we were teenagers, but why not buy a black negligee, a bottle of *Arpège*? Rarely, in all those years of Harriet and Al growing up, could we lie naked, with us sleeping in the living room, and Harriet running in when she heard a moan, and Al coming home late. Marty and I had learned to make silent love, not that either of our kids suspected, as far as we knew, that their old-fogey parents had anything biblical going on below the blankets. His face, his mutilated side had healed but never filled in. We rarely kissed all those years afterwards, but his fingertips caressed me in so many ways and his strong arms held me. His muscles, so weakened in the hospital, had firmed as he'd made himself walk farther, after friends got him playing handball at the Jewish Community Center, after he carried all our groceries up the five floors to our apartment, hauled the bags of laundry up and down.

I'd be lying if I said we didn't bicker, if I said all sex was perfect, that some of that fresh interest didn't taper down, that he didn't snore, that all the odors were pleasant, that his head on my chest didn't get heavy, that neither of us slobbered.

But those nights, blessedly together, alone in the apartment, the upright fan drifting a light breeze over us, I reached for Marty's sheet and covered his body, his healthy body, the way a sculptress drapes her work of art.

Diagnostic

Dana Koster

Does the buzzing of a phone line ever strike you as beautiful?

If, at a party, you stand in a group of five or more people
do their bodies sway in your direction?

Doesn't that dress look amazing on you?

Keeping in mind that you store and filter multitudes, which organ
would you say you resent the most?

Have you noticed a decreased need for sleep?

Do you want to sing?

Tell me about your urges. If I slide my tongue across your foot's
flagrant arch, shudder a breath against it, will I elicit goosebumps?

Would you describe yourself as a risk-taker?

Why not?

Two Tales from the Japanese

Michael Mejia

The Written Face

From the journey to the purchase, her voice had trembled with a mixture of anxiety and relief. Reiko came into the depths of the grove. Her pulsating flesh, reading between 15.2 and 47.5 microsieverts per day, blushed a faint red. She might have been panting.

My husband never came home last night.

It's not as though he's really gone missing. She won't talk will she?

He thinks it's a set-up.

Imagine! I led her by the hand behind a bush.

So what you're saying is, if I could bring these off successfully, even people who are not directly concerned, who have no interest in him, even though they have never even met, could be sent down the river? Are you sure?

I could see we'd have to provide some canned memories to convince her that the child was not hers. *Let's wait until evening.* Until then, I didn't want to miss the party. *Listen! The sound of a koto! Will you live this life?*

There was a hardness to the way she used her hands, as would village children coming home from school. They waltzed and tangoed the entire length of my nuclear subject. This distinct style, devised by Po Lo-t'ien about sixty years ago, is even more effective than picturing your legs expanding and contracting in stockings or Jōchō seated beside the well-kindled charcoal brazier taking it up in his hand.

Talk! Teach it to speak.

Who's your tow rope?

You are! You are!

I am not. Yoko is. Yoko! Oh, Yoko! Throughout my body, the complicated steps of the dance repeated and repeated, like boiling water running the distance around my hollow Chinese reactor—one of the two most powerful in the city—growing terribly behind an opaque ring of walls I built to protect you from my present feeling, which, honestly, is usually served more informally. *No boys allowed here!*

I was in a state! The inconsistency of her face! Who was this urban artist eating my dense city center, the most splendid there is, according to Kazuki? Its age did not even bother her. Not at all! I dodged here, there, but she kept on slashing at me!

I do feel good.

Komako asked me to bring this.

I might have to scale a wall at any moment! My legs had gone. I couldn't stand. *If I don't make it to that wall....* So kind, she crouched, heeding my dog's plaintive cries. The release down a woman's throat heard in this quiet environment is poetically called "the wind in the pines." Reiko had never before tasted such an amount of home essence, the capital's entire telephone book, candies from each district, each populous neighborhood, collected from the Serizawa Research Laboratory's recently conducted sessions, and arranged simply, like liquid medicine, except for one drop, which I saved for Yoko. Oh, Yoko!

This is the first time anything like this has happened: all those Tokyo addresses spread circularly on a thin face on the evening of the full moon of the eighth month. The strangeness of this combination would be news.

It was kind of you to come. She thought about finishing off the leftovers on her eyelashes, then, remembering her manners, found time to lightly touch up her face because that's what cute little cats do.

The air! I noticed that it had finally stopped raining. Soon, the roar of explosions surrounded the Fuji Hotel. The sufferings of the people there, however, were not entirely in vain.

Millions of Bodies

Air raid drills had begun all over the nation. My mask was flawless. The lieutenant kissed my lips nonchalantly and smiled so handsome a smile that his men felt rather inadequate. I looked like some medical person from far off Sinai who spoke little or no Japanese. It was March 23rd and he had no eye pain, no other pains. His symptoms probably still fell within the preatomic norm. He didn't even notice that his vision was odd, that he'd aged so!

There was a beauty in that moment. Just three days after the party at Fuji station, after wedging my dog as far as the eye could see into the depths of both his daughter and his third son, I came to on top of the first grandchild, twenty years old and home awhile from Ohira. I complimented him on his stubbornness and rigidity then fell unconscious again. Let me say this: Something like that—his cries, my total freedom, the darkness at the margins calling me to answer it, to eat its smooth substance—this gift that made such a difference to him should be videoed and meditated upon. When soup is served by the wind, flop down and bow to her! That's something somebody told me, actually.

Quietly, he inhaled the smell. The sound of the lieutenant's happy-go-lucky wife going about her work making wigs from the hair of the dead came to us, faint as the wind in the legendary pines of Onoe. At that time, Tokyo facilities only permitted twenty bodies to be burned per day, so there was none of the usual joy of an autumn harvest. We walked about the foot of that mountain with the air of two young women of China, inspecting corpses that were already waking up to move off in droves, half-dragging their legs, in the direction of Hiroshima. Fujinishiki went down to help Zeami count the officers. Tanomogi, a man of original ideas, remained motionless, his face turned away. He seemed to be suddenly taken sick. Komako cocked an eye at him.

At my word of command, the skipper and Kuniko helped out, unthinking, ungrudging. I told them there was an old mound quite close by this neighborhood to which they might take the bodies, and they began to load the things onto the canvas stretchers. The corpses shook their heads and bodies violently.

There must be some here who are food. Nan'ami hadn't eaten anything since last night, so the whiteness of starvation wasn't far from his mind.

We're wondering how you'd feel about waiting until tomorrow morning, one of his friends taunted him. The others pulled out a heap of stretchers.

Why don't you let me check on that? I didn't know what to think. I didn't see him as the embodiment of evil. His left hand, edged with black fur, was numb, as if it was ice. It wouldn't move and those who are superfluous remain behind, a principle by virtue of which there has been no famine in the country since the year before my time at the hot springs with his wife, submerged for two days in a numbered bamboo vase. It seemed only a matter of time before he also would appear on a table in Kobe.

A radiant moon had come out. *The look written on these faces mirrors a special knowledge of the curiously disparate trajectories of the heart usually managed only by Western sleeper films!* Kazuki brought his own face closer.

That assumes an Orient buried in the necessary self of Tokyo, taught to us by Japanese food, mothers, and printed culture.

Kawabata started to say something until the air pistol in my pocket gave him its regards. We set a rule to get angry. *The* chanoyu *entertainment is over!*

Suddenly, Dr. Soseki, the veterinarian, realized that Tanomogi had crossed to the other side. His body rose gently into the air, and I went after.

Long Life

JJ Chen Henderson

It is hard to wear hats in the wind,
but the old men in Beijing are stubborn.

Their jackets seem too large
on their shrinking bodies,

their eyes shrewd, like those
of Northeastern China wolves.

They shuffle forward, hurriedly,
as if being chased—they know

they can be caught up
by the time on their wrists,

and they have short legs.
They remind me of my aging father

in Texas, walking in circles
in a nursing home. I can't help but follow

these Beijing men, this one carrying a bag
of roasted chestnuts, that one with a roll of calligraphy

tucked under his arm. To the alley,
where the mimosa blossoms sway

like purple lanterns, and up the hill,
where the dragon dances at a festival.

They will, like my father, soon end
up on the fast road to another world.

They will come back,
a monk at a Buddhist temple tells me,

giving me a bracelet of *shu zhu* prayer beads.
Sometimes it feels a little too loose to wear.

SHUCKS!

Café con Leche

Joanna Lynne Ponce

La Maestra taught us Spanish in the small classroom downstairs. We were twelve, eleven mujeres and one hombre, y La Maestra, so that made thirteen really. She was light skinned, pocha like me but impossibly thin as if she dined just once a day on parsley and apple slices. Her hair was honey blond, rubia falsa was what I guessed, and she wore it back in a tight bun which gave her the look of a woman who was pretty much tired and fed up with all the nonsense in the world. La Maestra came from Colombia, and the way she said Co-*lom*-bi-a, said it with those Spanish Os so round and perfect, well, you could get swallowed up in one of those gigantic Os, get swallowed up and be lost for good.

It was junio, the first week of summer. Spanish class was downstairs in the adult community center. Even though Spanish class was in the evening, the air in the downstairs classroom, the Birch Room, was stuffy warm and damp on my arms. We sat in these plastic and metal chairs with fold-out desk tops. The chairs were hard and because the class went on for two and half hours mis nalgas often got numb and so did my foot if I kept my legs crossed.

The whole thing about me taking Spanish was my Spanish was caca. Really. I mean I could greet los clientes at the bank where I worked; *buenos días* and *cómo está* them and toss out the *adiós* as they left. We had a few viejas who wanted to charlar and all while they cashed la paga from their dead esposos social security. Everyone looked to me at the bank when that happened. Me? I'd just shrug my shoulders like what the hell do you expect me to do?

The truth was Amá didn't want us speaking Spanish at home. So we kids never learned it well, as my English teacher would say. Amá spoke only inglés to Marta, Junior or me the whole time we were growing up.

It was Abuelita who spoke Spanish all the time, because Abuelita knew less inglés than we knew Spanish. And Abuelita would not have Amá, her own daughter, speaking the language of the gabachos in her house.

When we traveled to Visalia, we always stayed with Abuelita even though her house was too tiny for us all. In the morning, Abuelita cooked us chorizo y huevos, and there were always fresh tortillas. And the best part of all was the café con leche which was really just a little coffee in a deep mug of hot foamy milk. Abuelita's café con leche served up in big round coffee mugs. I liked to sit under the kitchen table, on the yellow linoleum kitchen floor, and blow the steam from the cup, and watch the legs of Amá and Abuelita, and listen to them charlando though I understood nothing.

After Abuelita died, nobody spoke Spanish anymore. It was like Spanish had died, too. Or maybe it was there in Abuelita's tiny yellow house under the kitchen table along with the last of the café con leche, but we never went back. Amá had us kids to raise and she never cared much for Visalia anyway.

It was Mr. Richards, my boss, who told me I had to take Spanish classes. Mr. Richards, the managing director at the bank called me into his office. He's a tall, thin, blue-eyed guero and looks like a bank manager in his blue suit, fat red tie and silver cufflinks.

I show up at his office and he smiles at me like we're old cuates, points at one of the chairs in front of his desk, and tells me to take a seat. The chair is much smaller than his with a tiny rounded back that never lets you get quite settled. I sit down in the small chair, and I pull the hem of my skirt over my knees when I see Mr. Richards' eyes going that way.

Mr. Richards tells me he is recommending me for a promotion, but really it's just a change in my job description. He wants to add Spanish speaking teller to my job. He says how we have more and more Spanish speaking clients and how he wants me to be there for our clients, and to handle all the Spanish correspondence for the bank. I never heard anyone say Spanish so many times in one morning as Mr. Richards did.

I'm looking down at the hem of my skirt because a thread's come loose, but I'm careful not to pull at it. Instead, I say, "Mr. Richards, my Spanish is not that good."

Mr. Richards digs two fingers behind the knot of his tie and tugs to get it loose.

"What do you mean, Emma?" he says.

That's how I tell him about growing up not speaking Spanish except for when I went to visit Abuelita which was only a couple of times a year.

What Mr. Richards says to that is, "No problemo."

I don't tell Mr. Richards, the big jefe of our bank, that *no problemo* should be *no problema*. What I do is tuck that thin black thread back under the hem of my skirt.

Mr. Richards says, "I'm sure you can take a refresher course somewhere, just not during work hours." Then he says it's the end of our 'little meeting'. I can tell by how his eyebrows are all scrunched that we are no longer cuates. He pulls back his shirt cuff to check his watch and he's out the door ahead of me, late for something más importante.

With La Maestra and me it's like a Mexican *lucha libre* from day one. Only neither one of us is wearing a *lucha libre* mask, but it's obvious there's no love lost between us. If I raise my hand, she makes like she doesn't see me. When I'm busy looking something up in *el diccionario*, she calls on me, and I have to ask her to repeat the question, and then I have to remember to say *por favor*. There'd be this hardly a smile at all just at the corner of her mouth, and the dark in her eyes nearly black, and she'd repeat the question back at me in that fast, fast Co-lom-bi-an Spanish with those deep round Os and all I could do was blink back.

That first week after class, I did not sleep so well. I had dreams about La Maestra. Only it was Saint Agnes Catholic School all over again with La Maestra being Sister Ignatius, and me being twelve year old Emma Castillo. Only I was never Emma when I was twelve. I was Edward, named for a father who didn't stay around long enough to know me. And I was a boy with short wavy hair, thin as a rail but fast because when I got off the bus in a Catholic school uniform, I was a target for all the *Pachucos* and *Bloods* up and down East Fourteenth Street. So, I learned how to run when I should have been learning to speak Spanish so that twenty years later I'd be able to hold onto my bank teller position.

I guess I got kind of upset when Mr. Richards let me go in the fall. I didn't cry or nothing. Not there in front of the jefe and the other tellers. Canta y no Llore as the song goes. What Mr. Richards did was hire a nineteen year old chica who was totally fluent and who wore her skirts extra short and didn't mind Mr. Richards' checking out her legs all the time. And me, I'm training her at my job thinking the whole time that she's going to assist me.

Okay. I was pissed off majorly. I remember writing vete a la chingada on some note paper and stuffing it into the company suggestion box. Vete a la chingada!

For a week after I got sacked, I sat around in my apartment not even going out to buy more milk for my coffee when it ran out. And being home so long in that pinche apartment only made me more depressed. Me with no job and full of so much anger at La Maestra, and Mr. Richards and even those pachucos and bloods that had made my life a misery. And the one good thing being I no longer had to take Spanish class.

The very next thing I find myself doing, the thing that even surprises me at the age of thirty-two, is I'm making a phone call to Amá who I haven't talked to in I don't know how long. When she picks up the phone it's her same soft, dry voice saying, "Hello. Castillo residence." And it's the first time I hear it. The first time ever and for a moment I'm without words. Slight as it is, almost indiscernible, except me being her hija, I know mi Amá. What I hear is the very thin accent in her voice. Something she has let slip back in after all these years, now that she is older, maybe even too tired to care who might hear, an accent now over the phone as Mejicana as my dead Abuelita.

What I say next is "Amá, it's Emma."

"Emma?" my mother says and her breath over the phone makes my own face all tight and even my throat so that I can barely speak.

"Yes, mom. It's me, Emma."

And there we are talking on the phone, mother to daughter, like we'd done it every day of our lives. And Amá is all oh, Emma this and dear, Emma that and when am I coming to visit? And it's Amá talking, but it's Abuelita's voice gone south of the border and not once, not one time, does she call me Junior.

I Am Thinking About Calling Her

Vandoren Wheeler

I forgot the smooth weight
of a payphone receiver.

Its dial tone sounds
like *mmmmmmmm...*

I am jealous of her
slim, plastic cellphone speaker,

of its access to her
intricate ear folds.

Her ear. I think
of its lobe's tip

in my teeth
like a lentil.

Maybe after her *Hello?*
I'll close my eyes, whisper,

so I can imagine her
instinctively leaning

forward toward mysterious
me, the nubbin of her

left ring fingertip plugging
out the world to listen

to whatever the unknown

might say next…

She Could Be Anybody

Kim Chinquee

At the Falls, she sits along the water, seeing a mom with mangled hair, her tangerine shirt with holes and spots, a toddler on her hip who seems to want to do a backflip.

She rests on a bench where she sat once with a famous man who'd taken many efforts to see her.

She likes to come here, watch and walk and write. Next week, she'll get on a train to ride for many hours to see another man she used to be fond of.

She hears the woman-mom. The mom calls her baby peanut. The baby bawls incessantly.

She almost asks the mom if the mom needs help, but she knows, from those days when her son was two and three, and even twenty, no one can replace a mother, even when a child refuses to call his mother Mother.

As the mom walks away with her baby, she starts to think maybe the baby isn't the woman's child at all, maybe she's a hired nanny, or the baby's grandma, aunt or cousin. A girlfriend of the father, or a friend.

She remembers a time coming here with yet another ex and his young daughter, the man walking ahead and taking pictures, while she watched the girl run up too close to the water. It had been so cold, their breaths like beings of their own. She remembers the ice—its layer on the trees and benches, them crunching through the snow—like a protective blanket. Everything so cold. Then still.

She begins to walk along the stream, hearing the steady constant flow. She takes in the breeze. She stops. She feels the rail, and leans.

MTV Poem #15
Color Me Badd, *I Wanna Sex You Up*

Daniel Romo

George Michael, Kenny G, and Milli Vanilli walk into a bar… Trying to look hard in front of a tattered brick wall never works. Perhaps because hoop earrings that dangle like limp wrists are the antithesis of masculinity. Watching a videotape of a music video is more arousing than porn. Big Brother (who looks like a Sasha) watches everything you do in an elevator. Hence, blondes who resemble foreign love interests in spy movies make terrible night watchmen. Sitting on a man's lap leads to sex. Kissing a neck leads to sex. Men who tweeze their brows leads to sex. I was a virgin throughout high school because I never straddled a backwards metal chair, showing I could take charge of my love life. Despite trying to look comfortable, it's obvious that some men don't belong in the boardroom. Dance in your office. Dance under a bridge. Dance because the black man is the worst dancer in your predominantly white group! Friends who have sex in different locations at the same time can be colored any adjective they want. Why is front-of-the-limo sex never alluded to? Is there such thing as wanting to sex someone down? Sometimes, it's about nothing more than sex.

50 A.D.

Ben Slotky

Last weekend at the zoo, all the lemurs were throwing up. All of them, all the lemurs, all at the same time, all throwing up. I saw this and I thought to myself and maybe out loud, I thought so many lemurs, I thought so much throwing up. This happened, you can look it up somewhere, and this is what I thought or said or both when it did. I thought so many lemurs. I thought so much throwing up.

There could have been ten of them, ten lemurs, ten lemurs at the zoo, at my zoo, at the zoo in the town where I live. A lemur is a monkey; you know what ten is. The zoo was in Bloomington, Illinois, where I live, where I am. I am here right now and have been most of this whole time. Most of my entire family was watching them. My wife and I and our three boys were there. Our fourth boy wasn't there yet; we didn't know about him. My brother and his wife were there with their two kids. Their kids are my niece and my nephew. I think of them now and I wonder if they have any idea who I am. My brother and his son may be gay; my sister-in-law has a history of mental illness in her family. Her brother tried to stab her father, tried to kill him. This happened, and we were all standing there, the people I just said were, looking at animals, watching animals, look at them go.

We were at the zoo, all of us were, the whole family, the whole zoo. We were standing in the monkey house, just standing there looking, looking at the monkeys. There are worse things. We heard a wet sound, a wet slapping sound. A sound like soup, like buckets and buckets of soup being dumped, being slapped, being wet. Hot soup, wet soup, splashed soup, and if there was a place you could look up wet bucket sounds, where you could look up a sound, a wet bucket sound and this sound, that sound, that sound we heard, all of us, that is what it would sound like, like that, like that.

So we looked, we looked, and some of us looked up and some down and some around and maybe to the side and all of us, all of us, ended up looking at the lemurs. That made sense because the lemurs were all throwing up. Us looking made sense, and we watched them do this, all of us did, because what else were we going to do. We were going to not watch these lemurs throw up? I don't see how this could happen; I didn't then and don't now, because it can't happen, it couldn't have happened, you couldn't have not watched these lemurs throwing up, so that's what we did. We watched one then two then three then ten lemurs throw up.

They made sounds like *BLAAAH*.

They made sounds like *COUGH*.

They made sounds like *CARTOON*.

I pointed and made a sound like *AAAH*.

My nephew who is a boy but looks like a girl, he pointed and made a sound like *EWWW*.

My kids, my wife, other people, they pointed and made sounds.

I'm guessing there is something wrong with these monkeys.

This is what *I* said when we were done making our sounds; I said this out loud. Everybody seemed to like this; this was a funny thing for me to say after watching all of that. This is the type of thing I do, saying funny things is. I do it sometimes, I do that sometimes; I'm doing it now. After the lemurs made their sounds and we made our sounds, I said, "I'm guessing there is something wrong with these monkeys."

Good stuff, good stuff, thank you, small nod, real quick.

I bet even the lemurs would've liked this, liked what I had just said. I'm thinking about it right now. I envision a lemur who has just finished retching and heaving and slip-slapping soup out of his monkey mouth, his lemur mouth. I envision this lemur wiping remnants of vomit off of his furry mouth with his the back of his furry hand and hearing me say this, hearing me say I think there is something wrong with these monkeys, and looking up at me and being like yeah. His monkey eyes would be red from the throwing up. He'd blow some monkey air out his monkey nostrils and give a tiny monkey snort.

He'd be like you ain't kidding.

He'd be like I hear *that*. This lemur, that lemur, the lemur I'm talking about in this particular scenario, would kind of nod at me when this happened, a small lemur nod, and he would say those things I just said he'd say. That is exactly what would happen if that happened.

That would happen.

I was serious though when I said this, though, as funny as that is. I think there is something wrong with these lemurs. That is just my guess; I am no zoologist. [Looking up]

Real quick; a thing I am often asked is, "How much of these stories are true?" That is a thing I am asked and it is a thing I am asked a lot, sing-song. This comes up a lot more than you'd think, and I'm saying this not really knowing you or how much you'd actually be thinking about something like this; why would you? Why would you have any idea or ever have thought about how many times I'm asked about if these stories or real or not? Who am I even talking to, and it's bright up here, all alone. But no, I can't, I honestly can't see how it makes any difference. [Walking slowly, scratches head] The real answer is, doesn't really matter, who cares, same difference, next question. [Smiles, nods] That's the answer and it's good, it's a good one, that answer is, and a true one and a right one, but that's not the point, really I don't think, and that's not the point at all. The point is this. The point is that what I am about to tell you, the story that I am about to tell you, the point is that this story is absolutely, 100% true. Nothing's made up, and it's important we get that out, you and I do.

So we should start this out, and I know it looks like we've already started but we really haven't, by saying I don't feel comfortable making a lot of bold statements. It's true, I don't, I mean yes, I know, I know I sometimes say some wild things, some bold things. I have been known to state things, sometimes boldly. I have made bold statements and am prone to do so. This is not being disputed, here. I am saying I don't feel *comfortable* making bold statements. I'm saying it out loud, to you, to me, to monkeys. I know some of the things I say are kind of shocking and out there. I have been told that they may or may not be commercially viable; I know, I've been told that, I got that in a letter the other day. I got that in a letter from a literary agent who had requested to see more of my work. This guy discovered that book *The Lovely Bones*, which I never read, but saw the movie. Stanley Tucci. What I'm getting at here, is that this isn't what I'm saying, none of this is. What I'm saying isn't bold, what I'm saying or am about to say isn't. This isn't some wild conspiratorial rant about Jews or 9/11 or Freemasons. This is not something about chicken or black cherry cough drops or pepper steak or sharks. It's not about Tom Petty or anything like that, I will write about that later on. There will be plenty of time to talk about all of that, believe you me is what I will say and write right now. Plenty, plenty, but now is not about that. Now is about zoos, now is about otters. [Looks down]

In the spring of 2008, an otter died. The otter, whose name was Chloe, died at Miller Park Zoo, in Bloomington, Illinois, the town where I live, where I was, where those lemurs threw up near my boys and brother and niece. That was just setting the stage, the lemur-vomiting was. That was me using lemur vomiting to set the stage, the tone. It is effective; that is why you see so much of it in so many other stories, so many other acts. It is a trope, I think, ma'am, and the otter dying meant a lot to me for a few reasons, one of which is that I love otters. I do and I do. They are probably my favorite animals; you could ask my boys, they will tell you. Here is an actual conversation I had with my friend once, my friend who looks Jewish but isn't.

Anyway.

Here is what I said about otters; I said this.

I said, "Hey, which do you like better hippos or crocodiles?

I bet it's crocodiles. I like otters the best. They are nature's clowns. Clowns are also nature's clowns, only not as wet. Unless they spray themselves in the pants with seltzer water. Then they are wet. Clowns and otters are nature's clowns."

I said that, to my friend who looks Jewish but isn't. This was before the otter died, this is just a conversation we had.

I can't recall exactly when that conversation happened, that one just there did, I could look it up, could seek it out, but I won't and I wonder why not. I wonder, because it would be easy for me to do so. You can do things like that pretty easily, find out when you wrote things or find out when a thing happened. You'd think this would make things easier to understand, wouldn't you? If you could put a time and a place on it, if you could identify what it was and when it happened, you should be able to really understand a thing, right? That makes sense, so here's a thing that happened and here's when it did. On Thursday April 10, 2008, Chloe the otter died. She died at Miller Park Zoo in Bloomington, Illinois. She died of tumors that were growing in her stomach. That much I do know and you can look it up.

And I know what you're saying. You're saying otters die, Ben.

You're saying they die all the time, every day.

You're saying that's life.

You're saying this kind of softly, kind of quietly.

You are kind of wincing when you say this; you are wondering if I get it, if I understand this. You are watching me standing here looking at you. You are wondering if I can see you.

You are feeling sorry for me.

You're saying otters die, Ben, and you've said that twice now. You're saying an otter died right now, just now, right in front me, right while you were reading that last paragraph. You are holding this dead otter up right now. You are standing up, you are waving it in my face. You are angry. This otter is dead you are screaming! Why don't you grow up you are screaming and I hear this and I know and I agree. This is the world we live in, we live in a world where otters die, and it would be stupid and silly of me not to admit this, and I know this, so you can all just sit back down. [Looks up, timidly. Eyes wide. Expectant. Hesitant] And can I just jump in here? Let me, and we'll get back to this otter story, we will, but I need to get this part out first and if clear my throat here, right now, then I'm just clearing it, it isn't, it's not [smiles].

Ahem.

When I was 28 years old, I decided to open a movie theater. This is what I thought I would do back then and I have either written about this before or will write about it later, doesn't matter, how could it? I was very famous in my town, in Bloomington, Illinois for this. I bought a building. It used to be a movie theater. It was full of junk. You couldn't move in it. My brother and I saw a movie there once, *Superman 2*. Somebody stuck gum in my brother's hair. We were sitting in the balcony. We were kneeling before Zod. And that part there, ma'am? That could take forever, forever, and I am smiling now thinking about it, about how it could take forever to tell, but that's not what this is, this part isn't. I bought that building and spent about a year knocking things down and cleaning things out of it. There were so many things in this building. People would take pictures of me moving stuff out of this building. I would lift things and throw things and tear things down; I did this for months and months. Everybody watched, the whole town did, and I'm going to stop here, for a second I think. [Pausing, stopping. Hand with mic wiping forehead] You know how you sometimes stop for a second, ma'am? And what's the deal with [smiling, smiling in the light]. Ha. And this has gone so well, I think, so well. And I'm happy, I really am, that it turned out this way. I really am. And now, what I'm going to do, if it's ok [smiling now, leaning now, appearing genuine now]? Smile, and I'm going to not read from this anymore, from *this* book. I'm not going to finish that otter story yet, I don't think. I'm not sure I should. The otter dies, ma'am. It dies because they thought it was pregnant, right? Everybody did. She was on the front page of the paper; there was a web cam. Everybody was very excited, except–tumors! Not babies, tumors! As it turns out, tumors! Yeah, she died, Chloe did, because her stomach was riddled with tumors. We all watched. [Pause.] I know. That is nothing, right? We don't want to read *that* do we? Because all I'd do there is draw parallels, right? You know how you sometimes draw parallels? You know how you sometimes put things in brackets? No, I'd be like everybody watched this otter slipping and sliding around just like everybody watched me hooting and hollering around building a movie theater. Everybody was like "Aren't they *cute???*" Right, and yeah, and meantime, I'm dying, ma'am. Dying right in front of everybody, dying like an otter with stomach cancer. So yeah, no, I'm not finishing that. I'll read from my next book. That one's about work; that one's called *The Hill I'm Going To Die On* and this story's called "Larry Is a Hawk," and I'm going to tell you, [smiling, biting side of tongue] I'm going to tell you, this is as good as I can do it, right here, this transition [pausing, looking, staring. Smiling, confident, looking down, reading] and you're going to walk into work one day, and you're going to walk in to where you work, and this is going to happen. And on the *floor*, you're going to see like three or four people that you work with and they're going to be lying down. On the floor. And they're going to be right in front of you as you walk in to your office, your bank of cubicles, to whatever it is, to wherever it is. To the restaurant, to the shop, and these people are going to be lying on the ground and they're going to be in circles. And they're going to be lying there, on their sides, with their hands touching their toes and they're going to be in circles and you're going to say "What are *they* doing?" to somebody. Maybe to somebody else who's standing there or maybe you just say it out loud to nobody, but you'll probably say it, you'll probably say, "What are *they* doing?" And you're just going to be asking really, there's not anything behind it, no judgment, nothing. You're asking what are they doing only because when you walked in to your office, to where you work, three or four people you know will be lying on the ground. They will be circles, and this is going to happen.

And somebody eventually will say, "That's what they *do*." When this comes up, about the circles, somebody will eventually say to you, "That's what they *do*." This is going to be an explanation, and it's not going to be a good one, and you're going to say, naturally, "What do you mean?" And the only reason you'll say this is because you won't know what they mean, what that person means, when they say that this is what they do. They lie on the floor in circles now? You don't understand what that means, so you'll say, "What do you mean?" because that's what you should say. What you are doing makes sense. So you're going to say, "What do you mean?" and they're going to say "That's what they do. They lie on the floor in circles now."

And you're going to say, "OK."

And you're going to say "Do *I* have to lie on the ground like a circle?"

And they're going to say, "No. They do."

And this is going to happen to you, happen to you where you work, and you may do something funny when you walk in, and this may happen. And you may do like a tire drill exercise, right? Like you may hop in and out of these circles, like some sort of drill, right? And you could make some kind of joke maybe, like this is like calisthenics. Like Mao would have all the people do calisthenics to start the day before work and this would be *your* calisthenics, and you're just running over these people who are lying in circles on the ground. And it's not going to be a great joke; it's not the best thing you could do, but you're going to be a little unnerved. You know this is a strange thing that seems to be happening, but there they are. Circles, these three are circles and that's what they do now, you've been told, so there that is, too and you're going to walk around at work and everything's going to look the same. Everything's going to be the same as it was yesterday and the day before. It's going to look like that and if you think about that at all later on, if you think about the circle-laying or lying, you're going to think that was an aberration, if you think of it at all, and you may not. Think about that, about how you might not ever think about that at all. And you're going to sit down and Larry, who sits next to you, is going to be in a cage. And he's going to be perched on his desk in a cage, Larry is, and you're going to say, "What?"

You know, because you're going to *have* to say something, because circles on the ground was bad; that seemed odd, but Larry will be in a cage now. Larry will be *perched* in a cage now and you're going to say to somebody, you're going to say, "Why is Larry in a cage?" You'll say that and somebody will answer you, they'll say, "Oh, Larry is a hawk."

And you're going to go "*Larry?*" And you really should say it like that, like you're surprised, like it's a question. *Larry?* Like of all the people you'd considered could be a hawk at some point, Larry's the most surprising out of them all. You don't have to do this, but you can.

And you're going to go "*Larry?*" And you're going to point? With your right hand? Like this? "Him? Larry?"

And they're going to say, "Yeah, Larry," and you're going to say, "is a *hawk?*" And they're going to go, "Yeah, he's a hawk now."

And you're going to go, "Huh."

And you're going to pause, and you're going to be like, "Huh." And then you may be like, "Hmmm." And you're going to go, "I didn't know Larry was a hawk." And in your mind you're going to be thinking this is crazy and this needs to stop and eventually this is going to stop. And this will stop, but for right now this is going on they're going to say again, slower this time, "Larry is a hawk."

And you're going to ask, "Do I feed him?" And you're going to see that they're getting mad at you for asking these questions. They are going to think you are making fun of them, of Larry, of the circles. You're not, not really. You are doing exactly what you should be doing. You are handling things well, but they're going to be upset that you're asking. And you're going to say, "Do I *feed* him?"

And they're going to say "He can feed himself!" and they're going to be indignant, and this is going to happen, and you're going to say, "No, no! No, no, I'm not, I'm *asking*!" And your hands may be up, and your palms may be outstretched. You may back up a bit, you may smile.

You're going to say, "I'm not making fun, no. You have to understand where I'm coming from." And you'll be right, and you'll say, "Understand where I'm coming from, because I don't, I don't know what's going on. I'm being honest I have no idea what's happening. Like I walked in today and four people were lying in circles on the ground? And I tried to you know, make a joke, like a tire drill? I said something about you know, about Chairman Mao, and now you know Larry? He's in a *hawk* cage. And I'm asking like 'what do I do' not because I'm trying to be condescending, here. I'm seriously asking." And this? This is exactly what you should do in this situation; you are handling yourself well.

And they're going to say, "You've never heard of *hawkies*?"

And they're going to say, "*You've* never heard of hawkies."

And you're going to say, "No. No, I've never heard of hawkies," and the only reason you're going to say you've never heard of hawkies is because you've never heard of hawkies. That's why you're going to say that ma'am, for no other reason. You're going to say you don't know about hawkies not for any ulterior motive; you have never heard of hawkies. And the first thing you'll think? When they say, "*You've never heard of hawkies*," like that, like almost accusatory, like you've never heard of this? The first thing you'll think is "*Have* I heard of that? *Is* that a thing I should know about? Do I know this? Is it, is this, you know?"

But you haven't heard of it, so when you say "I've never heard of it," you're being honest and they're going to be like "Why should *Larry*, who is a hawk, OK? Inside. If he *believes* he is, and *feels* he is, and in his head he is, a hawk? Then why should *he* have to *conform* and *live* in your non-hawkie world? Like why? Why is *your* perception of how things should be better than Larry's? What's the *difference*? And don't you kind of see my point?"

And you're going to say, "Yeah…"

And they're going to say, "Well you *shouldn't*, because it's stupid. It's a stupid thing to say and this whole premise is absurd and ridiculous. And me saying because that because Larry thinks he's a *hawk*, he should be able to perch in a cage; that's the exact same thing as saying I don't believe life exists until a child is born, and that? Ma'am, [holding microphone high above head, energy, confident, smiling, nodding]? I want to drop this so bad right now, because did you see that? Did you see how I got us back here, how we made it? This fits, ma'am, it does, it does, and call *back*!!

Rebecca at the Falls

William Jolliff

My daughter with a book in her pocket
loves caves. When we hike through
Silver Falls, she cares less

for the brilliancy that rains from heaven
than for the dark places,
lava chimneys where pads of moss

carpet holes the waters have carved,
and millennia of quiet crying drop
from the Cascades to the sea.

We hear drips, but she hears
the mountain's sorrow and pulls herself
up the face of stone, a ledge

where the tears have stopped to rest.
She's read enough to know how this happens.
She's reading everything now.

Every Faculty Centered in His Hand

S. Cearley

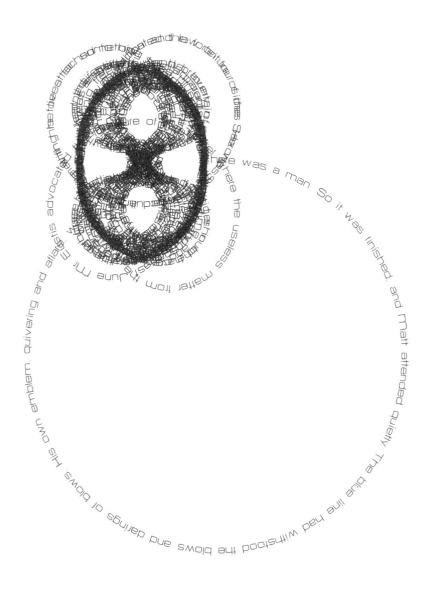

Sex and Death

Katherine Clarke Sinback

I discovered *Playboy* in Lee and Libby's downstairs bathroom. Lee and Libby, my next door neighbors, kept the magazines in a basket beside the toilet with a copy of *Better Homes and Gardens* on top, a flimsy shield against the curiosity of a ten-year-old girl. The summer before I turned eleven I spent many afternoons locked inside their bathroom, complaining of stomach problems so that I could take my time and fully absorb the images of the magazine. The pouting women in the photographs always looked a bit surprised to be having their picture taken while their bodies contorted in positions to emphasize the fullness of their breasts and the almost barren patch around their crotches. My father had once subscribed to *Playboy* but after my brother and I stumbled upon his stash among the boxes of Christmas ornaments in our basement and excitedly told our mother of our discovery, all remnants of centerfolds disappeared. I had no time to look at them, absorb the images, and figure out what this adult sex thing was all about. When I came upon Lee and Libby's *Playboys* I knew better than to mention anything to my mother.

Lee and Libby were the only couple living on our cul-de-sac at the end of Oak Glen Road who didn't have any children. Our piece of Oak Glen was populated by matching families—each had two kids born three years apart that fit neatly into three age categories. Being the only girl in the middle category, I strove to join the older set of girls, Donna and Lisa, who ruled all the other members of the Oak Glen kid-gang. The first summer after Lisa and Donna had entered junior high school, they no longer tolerated my presence in their circle. They turned up their noses at my foolish wishes to play kickball and kick-the-can and all the other games that we had once played until the streetlights flickered on and we were called inside.

"Go play with the kiddies," Donna said over her shoulder, too cool to even look at me.

Dejected yet still wanting to prove I wasn't the kiddie they thought I was, I holed up in my room and contorted my Barbie into some of the poses I had seen in the *Playboys*. Barbie tossed her head back and giggled seductively at Ken before I tucked them into the bed on the top floor of Barbie's dream house. What they did under those scratchy covers, I did not know. Donna and Lisa knew. Libby and Lee knew. I imagined smiling smugly alongside them, snapping my gum and giggling at secret jokes. I mashed Barbie and Ken together, expecting sparks, praying for revelation. Their plastic bodies remained cold, the smiles frozen.

Despite having no children, or rather because they had no children, Lee and Libby lived in the biggest house on our block. Their sprawling yard with all of its voluptuously shaped bushes and flower-trimmed borders was a testament to what people could do when not concerned with the complexities of child-rearing. Whereas Lee spent entire weekends clipping bushes, patting down mounds of sod, and planting begonias, my own parents considered a recently mowed lawn an award-worthy achievement. Even though Lee rarely spoke to us beyond a neighborly "hello," he invited us to use his yard and its many perfect hiding places during our games of kick-the-can as long as we didn't trample his flowers. Several of the trees were ideal hiding places, fat enough around that a kid could disappear, but I never considered hiding there.

I was creeped out by Lee and Libby. So different than the other suburban moms and dads, they were equal parts fascinating and frightening. Both were deeply tanned like they had been transplanted from Florida or California to our humble suburb of Washington, D.C. Libby was six feet tall with a skeletal physique. In the white-string bikini she wore to sunbathe on their back porch, she looked like a suntan lotion commercial refugee. The burnt-out, adult version of the big-eyed girls who gazed at me from the ballerina paintings in my room. All day she smoked cigarettes, played with her Great Dane, Beau, and waved at the neighbors on the block as they came and left their houses. In a world of buttoned-down mothers with their disapproving snorts, Libby was an oasis of wildness and glamour. But she also had this undercurrent of sadness that surfaced whenever us kids asked why she didn't have any children of her own.

Her cigarette-scarred voice was quiet and careful when she answered, "All you neighborhood kids are my kids. I couldn't have fun with you if I had my own." She drawled "my own" into a soft singular word, "ma-yone," the name of the little girl she didn't have.

We took only passing notice of the tears she blinked away before we resumed playing, high on sugar from the cookies she gave us straight from the cellophane.

The neighborhood moms were wary of Lee and Libby. They let us go over to watch movies, eat junk food, and admire Libby's porcelain elephant collection, but only in pairs. The summer of my exclusion from the older girls' club, I dragged my brother Max next door so that we could watch movies and so that I could steal away to pore over the *Playboy* I'd discovered the last time I'd borrowed their bathroom.

The inside of their house was exactly the kind of place I was sure I'd live in when I grew up. The leopard print couch matched the ceramic leopard statue which kept watch over the front hallway. Elephants of every collectable size and pattern marched in rows across the mantel and the shelves which clogged every space of wall where there wasn't a window or gold-trimmed tapestry. At the center of the room sat the huge television which showed the movies that Libby rented from Erol's especially for us. I sat frozen on the couch between Libby and my brother, afraid to spill anything on this decorated perfection.

The bliss of movies, cookies, chips, and sodas was only interrupted by my frequent bathroom breaks where I pored over the stack of bathroom Playboys. After a few minutes, I heard the shush-shush of Libby's calloused feet against linoleum.

"You okay hon? You need your mom?"

I flapped the magazine closed. "Just a few more minutes."

I had a hundred miraculous recoveries that summer.

During one of our midday movie marathons, I remarked that I wanted to go on a diet just like Lisa had so I could be skinny like Donna and Libby. To be on a diet was to join womanhood or at least teenage girlhood.

On our next trip over Libby unveiled a six-pack of Tab.

"This is what us dieting ladies drink," Libby said, unhooking the can from the plastic rings and slipping it into my hand. I felt a small rush in my gut. Diet sounded so adult. I imagined myself tan and thin like Libby, carelessly ruffling Beau's ears as I lay sunbathing in my yard. I slurped the saccharine sweet soda with glee until my eyes snagged on the warning label. *Saccharine has been proven to cause cancer in lab animals.*

My grandfather had recently died of cancer. Quickly I came to the conclusion that Libby was trying to poison us, specifically me. She couldn't have kids of her own so she was slowly giving the neighborhood kids cancer. I retreated to the *Playboy* bathroom, unable to gaze upon this month's playmate with the same interest. I felt an urgency to protect my brother and the rest of the kids from her poisonous soda. My mind raced with possible dark motives for their kind treatment of us over the years. The *Playboys* were part of a plot to draw me into a world I was too young to understand. They were a test to see if I would tell my parents. To see if it was safe to grant me entry into their twisted world. Everything that had once seemed glamorous about Lee and Libby turned sinister: the leopard, the gold tassels, even sweet Beau with her strings of slobber shimmering on her lips. What had been in those cookies?

After the saccharine discovery we mostly stayed away from Libby's plush living room. I retreated to my Barbies. From the bathroom window, I watched Libby sunbathe, still admiring her leathery tanned skin, but too afraid to go back. She seemed so sweet, so kind. I wondered if maybe Lee was the puppetmaster, forcing her to lure us kids to the house so that one day he could put his plan into action. When we passed their house, Libby waved at us and continued to invite us over to watch movies but suddenly we had better things to do.

In late August sun, the junior high school prejudice held by Lisa and Donna against me evaporated. I was allowed to tag along with them on their walks around the neighborhood as long as I didn't say anything. One evening I followed Lisa and Donna on their nightly walk and listened to their talk of cute boys and bitch girlfriends when Libby stepped onto her porch. Beau followed and sniffed around the yard while she smoked a Virginia Slim. She gripped the porch railing tight and wobbled a bit before settling back into a chaise lounge. Her eyes followed our path around the cul-de-sac.

When we got close to her house, she waved. "Girls, c'mere."

"Should we keep walking?" Lisa whispered to Donna.

"Nah, come on, let's see what's up," Donna said, thrusting her pointy chin into the air and sashaying ahead of us like a debutante.

Behind Donna, Lisa and I trudged up the long driveway to the porch. Beau greeted us with wet snurfles against our hands and sloppy licks on every sweaty spot on our arms. I directed all my attentions to petting the friendly dog, relishing the oily softness of her velvety fur.

"Pretty girl," I cooed softly, forgetting to act cool.

Donna rolled her eyes at my enthusiasm.

"What're you girls up to tonight?" Libby asked, her eyes half-open.

"We're just hanging out, you know, talking and stuff. It's no big woop," Donna said.

"Don't you all play kick-the-can no more? I remember when you used to hide behind our bushes. Y'all were so cute," Libby smiled lazily.

Lisa and Donna rolled their eyes at each other.

"Kick-the-can is so lame," Donna said.

I nodded while longing for the old days. Listening to Lisa and Donna's talk was nowhere near as fun as cutting through the humid summer air, fearing the touch of a friend's hand on your back as the chirp of crickets ushered in the night.

"You girls shouldn't grow up so fast, enjoy it while you can," Libby said, her speech slurred and her eyes out of focus.

Beau nuzzled Libby's hand with her huge head. Lisa, Donna, and I stared at the ground. All the creepiness I felt around Lee and Libby before bubbled up again.

"Wanna see what Lee's done to the side yard? It looks fucking great," Libby said as she struggled to stand from the lounge.

We all nodded. The sound of Libby's "fucking great" echoed in my ten-year-old mind. I'd heard Libby and Lee hurl insults at each other, peppered with "bitch," "fuck," and "goddamnit," a few times over the seven years we had lived beside them, but never had they said those words consciously in our presence. Libby's careless "fucking great" had broken some wall between the kid and adult world. I felt unprepared for this diet soda world with its cuss words and complications.

Libby led us around to the side of the house mumbling words that I couldn't understand under her breath. Every sentence I'd catch a "he" or a "shit" or some other small island of a word stuck in the sea of nonsense sounds. Even Lisa and Donna looked scared.

A door slammed behind us. I turned. My mom stood on our porch, her hands on her hips, her neck craning to get a better look at what was happening.

"Don't you bother Libby now," she called.

"We're not," I yelled back as Libby, Lisa and Donna turned the corner and disappeared from my mother's view.

When I rounded the corner, Libby was in a heap on the ground. Her legs jutted out from her slumped body at awkward angles, her sandals had slipped askew. The three of us froze. Libby's head flopped up, "I'm fine, I'm okay, don't worry 'bout it."

Lisa bent down to help. Libby hissed something in her ear. Lisa slowly raised up, her face a puzzle of shock.

Donna stared hard at her. "What?" She barked.

"She called me a whore," Lisa said.

Before I could run and get my mom, before Donna's mom could rush over from her porch, before Lisa's face could settle back into normal, Lee rushed out the door and pushed though the wall of girls surrounding Libby.

He told us to go home. Libby was sick, she forgot to take her medicine. She started to sob as he slipped his arms beneath her armpits and lifted her to standing. We watched the two of them stumble toward the door, Beau trailing them, until the door slammed and sent an echo around the cul-de-sac. When I got home and asked my mom why Libby called Lisa a whore, my looked away. "Because she is sick, very sick."

After the "whore" incident, Libby grew increasingly reclusive. The lounge on the back deck where she had sunbathed, slick with suntan oil and sleek as a fish, lay empty. When she let Beau out to pee in the front yard, she remained in the doorway, a shadow. As I got absorbed in my own adolescent whirlwind, Libby left my mind. After Beau died, Libby stopped leaving the house completely. Sometimes when a friend picked me up to go to a movie or when my boyfriend dropped me off from one of our late night prowls around the darkened playgrounds of the suburb, I'd glimpse Libby's form in the window. The curtain of their downstairs window pulled open until I looked in her direction. Then the curtain fell shut. I'd wonder if I had imagined the dent in the curtain.

I awoke on a December morning, my mind buzzing with French tests, Sex Pistols anthems, and the perfect Christmas gift for my first real boyfriend. My mom stirred her tea at the front table. My brother's place at the table didn't match the bowl of cereal and glass of orange juice that was set in mine.

"Where's Max?" I asked, ready to snort at what I assumed to be some poor excuse for getting out of school.

"He's sleeping. He was awake all night," my mom said. Her complexion was gray; her eyes tired. She looked at me. "Did you hear the sirens?"

Late in the night with the neighborhood asleep, Libby had climbed in the front seat of her car, sparked the engine and let it run until she was dead from carbon monoxide poisoning. When Lee discovered her, it was too late. The paramedics worked for an hour trying to revive her. Our neighborhood became a blur of flashing lights and confusion. My parents and my brother were awakened by the commotion and watched from the front window of our house until finally my dad went to investigate. They saw her thin form on top of a stretcher, covered by a blanket.

I held back tears and shoveled a spoonful of cereal into my dry mouth. I tried to go back to the morning I was having before Libby died when everything was about me and my world.

I remembered the time that I had gone over to Libby's house alone, before the saccharine incident, and I had told her one of my biggest lies. As I ate cookies and Libby took slow drags from her cigarette, I told her about how my extended family loved my brother more than me. My grandparents showered him with gifts because he was the first grandson in our generation. I was one of three granddaughters, nothing special. As a result I got crappy presents at Christmastime, things like flannel nightgowns and underpants. The next day Libby knocked on our door to borrow something from my mom. She also had something for me. I stood at the top of the stairway, hidden from view, as Libby quoted my lie to my mother. My mom said things like, "How interesting," and "Is that so?" She said nothing to counter my huge lie.

Libby left, and my mother came up the stairs. She handed me a pink ceramic elephant that I had admired in Libby's collection.

"A present from Libby," she said with a raised eyebrow.

We sat on my canopy bed, and my mom recounted the story, lie-by-lie. "Did you really tell her all those things," my mom asked.

"No, of course not," I said, rubbing the belly of the elephant. "She must be confused or something."

My mom nodded. "Okay."

I stuck the elephant behind a row of books on my bookcase, feeling guilty for getting away with my lie at the expense of Libby. Briefly I worried that I wouldn't be allowed over to her house anymore to watch movies and pet Beau. I forgot about the elephant and Libby.

That morning as I warmed up my car, I stared at Lee and Libby's house, replaying my lie over and over again in my head. Even as a kid, I had sensed Libby's weakness and sucked out what I could before leaving her. *Playboy*, diet soda, cookies, and *Superman*. Over breakfast my mom told me that Libby had attempted suicide many times before this one. Pills, slit wrists, and, finally, the car. Hearing that somehow made me feel better, like Libby had finally been successful at something she set out to do, but it was a hollow relief. I drove to school, and among the bustle of high school Libby turned into a story to tell my friends, something to make them say "That's so fucked up," before we rushed off to class. Suicide held a tortured mystique that I hadn't previously associated with Libby. I associated suicide with girls who dressed all in black and pontificated on the meaninglessness of the universe, or with boys who were picked on until they broke. Suicide seemed somehow too deep for Libby. She was too tacky for it. Too much *Playboy* and not enough Plath. And then, later, after theorizing about possible causes and crafting conclusions from the scraps of her life that I had witnessed, I was alone again with Libby and the feeling that I didn't understand anything, really.

The Scar

Noel Sloboda

My brother never once asked
about the sliver of white
where dad's teeth punched
through his chin years before.

Maybe heredity would have become
just one more excuse—
like the late filing deadline
or the ungrateful kids,

or the new war, or the old boss,
or the new boss, or the ex-girlfriend,
or the ex-boyfriend of the new
girlfriend, or mom with her collection

of Italian glass angels. Or me
with my constant questions; another cue
to twirl out from darkened wings;
another night balanced

on a barstool like some baby bird—
throat yawning—just waiting

for the worm to drop. Still,
even through that sweet

and sour tequila miasma
he must have sensed that second mouth
on our creator came from something
more than a spill in rough weather.

A Frame

John Yohe

As the elevator rises to the third floor
and rain sprinkles your past, you examine
the toad under the plastic truck and I try to
appear unconcerned with the age of your new
bicycle, because appearing in drag in the talent show
has left me exhausted
I know what this
means to you and your girlfriends and how simple
a grilled cheese sandwich should be to smell
at noon in a small A-frame house in the
woods at the end of a two-track, but instead
I think of dragonflies mating in flight and how
amber must feel cooling around the body. I know
you'll say that this is not in spite of everything
but because of it, but again, I don't know
your history, or even how to salsa dance, though I
would like to, with you, and get fat-free
yoghurt with almonds and pecans, though what you
said last night is true, or will be: out
here on the edge of things, being must be more
interesting than the center, which is still as necessary
as night and dreams

All of which makes me happy
to see you running barefoot in a skort, though I've
burned my fingers now, or will, and anyways,
your sister called. She said to say hello.

KinderGarten Crush

MR.WOLF! ©ARONNELSSTEINKE.COM

1/19/2014

Pets

Shane Hinton

All the animals I had between the ages of five and twelve died grisly deaths.

We found the goat eating glass off the floor of the barn. I pulled the animal to its pen and Dad nailed the fence back in place. The goat lay in the grass and was dead before the sun went down.

Our chickens were killed by a fox. I found the coop covered in blood when I went to feed them before school. My favorite one had an extra toe. The fox left her foot by the door of the coop.

My python wiggled out of his cage so often I had to stack dictionaries on the lid to keep it closed. He eventually knocked the lid off despite the extra weight. We found him in the attic when his decaying body stank up the house.

Our cat got an infection in her brain the same day I got suspended from school for fighting. She fell out of the oak tree in the front yard and broke her back. We put her in a cardboard box lined with paper towels, where she pissed herself until the vet put her down.

An alligator ate one of our dogs in a pond on the farm. For a while I carried a rifle to the pond every day and shot at bubbles in the water.

Another dog followed the tractor for half a mile drinking weed killer before anyone noticed. Dad held her head as she died next to the ditch.

We dug rows and rows of graves in the cow pasture, marked by small wooden crosses with each animal's name and date of death. The crosses would last a month or two and then get blown down in a thunderstorm or trampled by the cows. The earth over the graves sank in, leaving a series of shallow depressions.

Even without the crosses, I could tell which animal was buried in which hole by the size of the grave. I walked through the rows after school, trying to remember each of them individually, the way it felt to pet them, the different foods they liked to eat.

On the way back from the farm one day, Dad stopped the tractor when he saw me sitting by the graves.

"It's almost time for dinner," he said.

I was trying to remember the goat, so I didn't say anything.

"There's a litter of kittens in the barn. Maybe you can catch one."

I went to the tractor and sat on the wheel well. Dad drove to the barn and then cut the engine.

"Over there," he said, pointing to a small room in the corner of the barn filled with two-by-fours, engine parts, and rusted paint cans. I opened the door and listened for mewing.

My eyes adjusted to the dark. I lifted pieces of wood off the pile in the middle of the room and leaned them against the wall. Underneath a piece of plywood I found the mama cat lying on her side, looking sick. Seven kittens sucked at her teats. The mama's eyes had dried mucous in the corners. She didn't react when I reached in and picked up one of the kittens by the scruff of its neck. The kitten was white with a black Y shape on its forehead. I carried it out to Dad, who was greasing the tractor.

"Hawk attack," he said. I held the kitten in my palm. It nestled against my curled fingers and closed its eyes.

"Rabies," I said.

I sat down on an old tire and the kitten fell asleep in my lap. Dad pumped the grease gun until red grease dripped from the bearings, pushing old black grease out onto the floor of the barn.

War Paint

Nick Triolo

Boy stripes face
Deep with color
Lathered thick and slanting

He bursts outside through
Frail screen door
Heart tha da da dumping
Battle drum phantoms
Scouring hilltop mist moist

How else can I respond
But to fight them

Gnashed teeth spitting curses
Under breath
Bonfires for eyes
Boy fists rosebush battleax
Knuckled grip bleeding
Trembling

Charging up the hill
He screams he hates he burns

Infantries of grass
Part not for this
Commitment to carnage

But the enemy needs to die

When Boy finally reaches
The front lines the edge
All he finds is water
No ghouls no fire-heaving monsters
No fanged Krampus

Just water
Just placid hydroglass
Just him and Pond

War paint coagulant
Alchemizes with
Sweat and sorrow
Refractive confusion
Chest rising chest falling like
Leavened bread

Where are you
Boy's murderous voice
Fires sonic blanks in search
Of Other

Stripping clothes ripping
Boy hangs bleached underwear
On caribou antler velvet
And wades into Pond

War paint begins cascading
Preamble to rainstorm
Drips Drops Drips Drops
Technicolor tear after tear
Warbler yellow
Cobalt blue
And fireball red
Breached levees
Of swollen eyelid

And he collapses
He descends
Beneath Pond mirroring'
A young wiry composite
Heaped of bone and fat
Muscle and wound

Surrendered implosion

When Boy finally resurfaces
He has pond scum for hair
Lily pads for ears
Cattail spike for a nose
And minnows for lips

War paint is gone

So Boy leaves his old clothes
Abandons underwear hanging
Scribbling obey into
Wind's outstretched palm

He walks on all fours
With his cattail nose
His scummy hair
His lily ears
And his fishy lips
Back down the hill
Through grass infantries
Raising their blades high
In wild solidarity

Back home
Naked Light Free
Surrendered
Victorious

Scrimshaw

Robert Wrigley

With a scratch and some talon scrabble, the owl
lit upon the moose femur bird perch
favored most often by ravens and jays,
and stayed, slumping through the morning
against the porch post the bone was attached to,
as it began, slowly at first, then faster, to die.
Its chest feathers spread and its beak tucked
therein. Its left eye closed, then its right,
and at last it swung downward, its wings opened,
and it dangled by a pair of deadly claws
for a while. And the late summer breeze
swayed it gently, and the talon tips scored
into the bone a pair of half-moon scribes,
west and east, I sometimes, these years later on,
reach up to trace, and which sometimes
a raven will examine and decipher,
before cocking a head and cawing
then going on its way. This is my note
about those marks to whomever might one day
inhabit this space—curatorial, explanatory—
although weather's already dulled the etches,
and someday, long after I am gone,

if some more decorous tenant has not removed
the many baubles of bone affixed to posts,
walls, and fascia boards, it may occur
to him, or her—what with the bone's long microbial
gnaw and disintegration—that here is evidence
of what it was that killed the moose.
Let it be known it was not so.
Let it be known the owl dangled dead
another hour before the final unclench and fall.
Let be known I left its body where it lay,
and in the night something unseen and silent
bore it away.

Terror

Musical

Divorce Request

Vandoren Wheeler

After we quietly chewed
and swallowed our lunches

together in the center
of a strange restaurant

equidistant from her workplace
and our half-empty house,

she came back to me
from the bathroom,

trembling slightly, and showed
how she had ground

her unhappiness down
into the crude blade

of a single sentence—her

mouth its first wound—

Love Potion #369

Susan DeFreitas

I met Angela for lunch at our old place, across the street from the bio lab where we'd labored so long over ova. Hard to believe a decade had passed since last we'd huddled over those glowing, backlit ghost babies, looking vaguely yolk-like on their slides. We'd been grad students of Jeffries' then, trying to help him determine the effects of Fukushima's fall out on human fertility, even as we'd been sizing up our dates' DNA on the sly. How ironic now, that Angela and I—both of us pushing forty now—had emerged as some of the fittest researchers in the field of reproductive science, but so far, had failed to reproduce.

The name of the restaurant had changed since our grad school days, but the seating arrangement had somehow remained the same. We were sitting at our old table by the window. Angela ordered the chicken Caesar and inquired as to the chardonnay.

Our server shrugged and said, "It comes from a box." He looked all of seventeen, but Angela was smiling at him the way a full-grown woman smiles at a full-grown man.

"How's Jan? Have you heard from her?" she asked me. Watching him, somewhat creepily, as he walked away.

"Not since her last kid. What is it, the third?"

"And the senior researcher position?"

"Passed over for Patrick."

"Oh no, not the Prick!"

Why, I wondered, was Angela even bothering with this sort of miniscule biz? We knew all this already through Facebook and LinkedIn and the SheGeek WannabeMommies affinity group and yet had felt no need to contact one another in years. Why had she messaged me?

"Bailey," she said, finally. As if my very name, the fact of it, was adorable. "I have something to show you." She pulled a vial of vile-looking green liquid from her purse. Her voice segued to a whisper. "This," she said, "is the answer to our prayers."

"I'm an atheist," I reminded her.

"This," she continued, "is the answer to every woman's prayers." Sounding very much like a 50s era ad for a washing machine. "The alpha and omega of female desire. The killer app. The evolutionary game changer."

"All right," I said, "but it looks kind of gross." Like the mother of some sort of fungus trapped in a sample of pond water.

"Watch," Angela hissed. She popped a little button at the top of the glass tube and shook it, then dabbed whatever was in it on her wrists and behind her ears. It smelled like mint and caraway seed. Both of which, it occurred to me, contain mirror molecules of carvone.

"What is that stuff, exactly?" When I reached for the vial, she snatched it away, as if I were attempting to palm her latest high-dollar wrinkle eraser.

"On a scale of one to ten," she said, "how would you rate our server's current level of sexual interest in me?"

Our server was busy chatting up the busty little busser refilling ketchup bottles at the wait station. "Can we use negative numbers?"

Angela favored me with a withering glare. Or, at least, a withering glance. "Now," she said, "watch." And turned to our server's back.

It was if she'd blown a dog whistle. The kid turned around and looked at her. Angela favored him with her best come-hither, and in forty seconds flat, he was refilling her water glass.

"Ladies," said the kid, "I'm sorry your order is taking so long. May I interest you in some complimentary bruschetta?"

I checked my wristphone. It had been no more than five minutes since we ordered.

"Sure," Angela practically purred.

The kid smiled at her chest and sauntered back to the kitchen. With, I might add, some seriously skinny whiteboy swag. Now it was my turn to lean across the table. "Ang," I whispered, "what is that stuff?"

She smiled. Like the cat that caught the canary. Sat back, one Crossfit leg crossed atop the other. "You're the one who came up with it."

I had no choice but to greet this with a blank stare.

Angela popped the top of the vial, in and out. One could say a bit obsessively. "Marshall's? Late night take out? Bull sesh #369? You said the person who developed the tech that would allow a woman to be attractive to only the man she wants to be attractive to would one day rule the world."

"You seriously took notes on that?"

Angela looked at me like I was stupid. "Imagination can't be taught."

"All right, but—"

She lifted her hands, as if all of this should have been obvious by now. "Bailey," she said again, in a way I really don't like. "You have imagination. I don't. You know this."

"Sure," I said. "I mean, sort of. I know you always had trouble visualizing things. I guess I just didn't realize you were keeping notes on every single drunken conversation we had in grad school."

Angela waved this away, even as I wondered, what the hell else did I say under the influence of Marshall's $3 margaritas that this woman still has on file somewhere? It had been noted that Angela Edgers had a mind like a steel trap, and I was starting to worry I was going to have to gnaw off my own leg or something.

"Just try it," she said.

Cautiously, I took the vial in hand and popped the little button on its little green stopper, then dabbed a little of this exotic substance (the semen of the psychedelic bufo toad, for all I know) on my inner wrists.

"Now," Angela told me, her voice pitched low, "pick a man."

The only Y chromosome in the joint besides our server, as far as I could see, was a dignified older dude who appeared to be dining with his wife. "Any man?" I asked.

"Any man. Just imagine having sex with him."

I nearly choked on my wine. At the image of this old man and old dong, going to town. It was enough to put me off the rather delicious bruschetta that had recently arrived.

Still, it came, unbidden—the profoundly disturbing image of this grandfatherly fellow pumping away on top of me. When I looked up, he was staring at me over his wife's shoulder, smiling unsteadily, nodding in that way of elderly people who have lost the power to hold their heads still. He slowly dabbed his mouth with his napkin. Deliberately displaying, I realized, a high-end Omega wristphone that probably cost as much as my car.

"Jesus," I said.

"Do you understand the magnitude of this discovery?" Angela was leaning over the table, pressing my forearm, her dark eyes wide, and for once, all that over-produced drama didn't seem so over produced. "We're going to be rich."

"We?"

She looked at me like, duh. "I told you. This whole thing was your idea."

"Ang, any idiot could have come up with that idea."

Her eyes narrowed. And I could see immediately that this the wrong thing to say. Because it was true: Angela really had no imagination whatsoever. She was famous in our circle at U Chuck for being unable to imagine, for instance, what soda pop mixed with hot sauce might taste like, and as a consequence, had been forced one evening at Jan's to find out.

"Don't play coy," she said. "Remember Dr. Athena?"

"The crazy lady who advertised in all those magazines? Back when there still were magazines? Ang, I told you, she's not a real doctor."

"No," Angela agreed, "but you were right. She was on to something."

"So what? You just called her up, and she gave you her magic formula?"

Angela waved away this subject as if it were a bad smell. "Dr. Athena is no longer important. What's important is you and me. I want us to go into business together."

Wait. "What happened to Dr. Athena?"

"Bailey," she said, "pay attention. The Selective Attraction Formula is worth billions. Forget Senior Researcher at Ominous Omnibus. You can fund whatever the hell you want. Build your own lab. Hire your own staff. Cure crotch cancer, or whatever it is you've been trying to do."

"Cervical cancer."

"Whatever."

I sat back. As with any attractive offer from Angela, it made me suspicious. "How's this supposed to work? You want me to handle the stuff that's too boring for you?"

"I want you to handle all of it."

"What are you going to handle?"

Angela smiled. Very much the way she used to in o-chem, when she'd already figured out what would be on the test and already knew that she knew it. "Think about it," she said. "All I have to do is walk into any bar in Ballard on a Friday night and pick out the hottest man in the room. Ever since Omnibus, the neighborhood is crawling with virile, intelligent men with a ridiculous amount of disposable income. But you and I don't have time to chat them up and wait for them to ask us out, do we? Because we're up at six a.m. six days a week, just to keep up with those of our male colleagues gunning for the promotions. That's the beauty of the thing."

"The beauty of what thing?"

"Selective attraction. It's like birth control for dating."

"Ang—"

"No," she said. "Just listen. My biological clock is ticking."

"How old do you think I am?"

"One year, four months, and six days younger than I am."

"That doesn't mean anything."

Her face was pleading now. "Bailey, you'll have your kids when it's time. After you get the business established."

"Are you kidding? That could take years."

"Your eggs are still in decent shape."

"Excuse me? How do you know what shape my eggs are in?" Our salads were still sitting on the table between us, but somehow, I was on my third glass of chardonnay. Which is how I knew that if I backed down now, Angela would destroy what few eggs I had left—just sitting across from her at this table was so stressful I could feel my ovaries shrinking. The fact was, Ang was fine companion for clubbing and cramming a few nights a week, but I would sooner have committed myself to a lifetime of field research in Siberia than go into business with her.

"You know what?" I said. "No." And lifted my finger in the general direction of our server.

"Bailey, are you crazy? Do you have any idea what kind of opportunity I'm offering you?"

Not unlike all those times she offered me old clothes, old boyfriends, old lab partners she'd managed to piss off. I shook my hair loose from its sloppy bun. Stretched—a little asana mudra thing. And settled back in my seat. "Angela, do you know me? Like, even at all?"

"Of course I know you." Though she was looking right then like she didn't.

"I don't care about money. Or research. Or really even curing crotch cancer. All I've ever cared about is being really, really smart, and passing on my really smart genes. I'm not going into business with you."

Poor Ang just couldn't believe it. Clearly, she never imagined me turning her down. (Then again, imagining was never her strong suit.) She opened her mouth, but before she could express her shocked disbelief, our server returned. "Is everything okay?" he asked.

"The check," I replied, undressing him in my mind. I was still wearing the stuff, right?

"No check," said Angela, no doubt doing the same.

"Uh," said our server.

"Now," I said, with more force.

"No," Angela said with even more.

Our server was starting to sweat. I could see the beads of it forming on his fuzzy upper lip, poor kid. There might as well have been smoke pouring out of his ears.

"How would you like to impregnate my friend here?" I asked him. "She'd really like to make it with you. Maybe show you a thing or two."

The server looked like a deer caught in headlights—unable to move in the face of what he was staring at. Which, at the moment, was my chest.

"Actually," Angela said, "my friend Bailey here has been talking about your ass since we stepped in here. Would you like her phone number?"

He blinked. And cleared his throat. "Actually," he said, his voice pitched low, "I was sort of wondering if you ladies had ever considered, you know, a little—"

Which, as far as I was concerned, was more than enough. "Thanks for lunch," I said, standing up. "Good luck with Selective Attraction. And stay out of my files."

Angela looked the way she looked when denied anything ever, really—stunned. I wouldn't have put it past her to stand up with me, dine and dash, and maybe even force me into a headlock in the back alley. (Really. You never knew with her.) But now I was eying a cop on the sidewalk out front. Young, but not too young—and quite fit, I could not help but notice. Before I realized what was happening, he was smiling at me, a bit of a twinkle in his eye.

As I made a beeline for the door, the old codger turned, unsteadily, to catch a glimpse of my ass as I passed. I turned back and caught the watery eye of the old man's wife. "Watch out for that one," I told her.

Out on the street in the drizzling rain, it seemed the cop had stopped for a cup of coffee from the cart next door. No ring, I noticed, as he poured the cream, then the honey. Midtwenties or so. Prime time for the production of certain specialized cells.

"Excuse me," I said, suddenly all a'ditz. "Could you help me find my car?"

"Certainly," he said. "Though I'm about to get off." He cleared his throat. "I'm about to get off the clock."

"Well, then," I said, "we'll just have to make this quick."

I was thinking about helping the young officer out of his uniform, of course, but also about caraway and carvone. About sexual selection in birds, whose cheeky females get to choose. And suddenly, I could see all the men on the sidewalk decked out like peacocks, strutting their stuff as they passed—this hot young cop back at the lab, doing a fancy dance just for me. Just a little good old fashioned chemistry, but who knew what discoveries we might make?

Wet

Kim Chinquee

I move my arms in the water, the force of them like physics. I feel the waves of this Great Lake, different from the lakes that I grew up with. Though those lakes were quiet, they were static and feckless, filled with bugs, and I'd come out of them with leeches, my mom taking off my swimsuit. She'd have to get my dad. He was the one with the lighter who could burn them off. She told me to relax. She said it was easy.

The leeches were shaped like the bay leaves she used to put in soup. They were black, slimy, and though my skin is white, somehow they seemed native, as if they belonged there.

I was afraid of the lighter. But I was more afraid of my dad. And to say I was afraid made me more afraid than just being afraid. By then, I was practiced at focusing on other ways of pretending not to be there. My dad never really talked much.

Here, I feel the waves. I wear goggles, a cap, a wetsuit. I practice the front crawl, bilateral breathing, trying to feel.

Today the lake is thick. I stop and try to stand. To see where I am.

Suicide Doors

Lydia Netzer

She saw her future life stretching out before her, textured and beautiful. She would live alone in the country. She would sit and watch the sun come up every morning, the sound of bugs in August covering the ringing in her ears. She would have big fields and 10,000 horses. The man who cut her grass and mended her fences would laugh at how particular she was about everything to do with the animals. Clean stalls twice a day. A strict grooming regimen. In her drafty farmhouse, she would know exactly how much creamer was left in the red carton, and how many days it would last. The apple trees would bear such fruit the branches would break and the ponies would get fat from eating them off the ground.

She asked her agent: "What kind of book do I need to write in order to afford this beautiful life?"

"Try erotic short stories," her agent suggested. "You can sell them as one-offs on Amazon. Make a million."

She had two husbands and many children. The husbands were dead, but the children would never leave. They would grow old, wither, and die hanging off her refrigerator.

But for now, the apartment in the city buzzed with the sound of their living. It was an erratic buzz, and didn't cover the ringing sound. Not all the time. In the city, quiet had a different flavor, like an awkward interruption, while you were waiting for something else to make a noise. In the country, quiet could last for hours, and the interruption was the falcon cry, the thunder, or the sudden close whine of a mosquito, quickly stifled.

Picking through the living room to her office, she snagged a notebook and a pen.

"What," said her son, draped over her office chair, glued to her computer.

"I have to write a short story."

"On paper? What is this, 1986?"

"Someone is using my computer," she mentioned.

"Tell that person to get off!"

"Ok, will you get off my computer, please, so I can use it?"

"NO!" he shouted. Then he laughed his braying laugh and said, "Oh, mom."

She laid the notebook on the kitchen table and poached a perfect egg. It was one of her strange skills in the kitchen. With all the kids around all the time she had to keep it simple stupid with the food, so she developed these basic specialties. She knew how to add the exact amount of vinegar to hold the whites together, how to create a perfect vortex of swirling water in the pot, when to lift it out, how to make sure it didn't taste wet. In her future as a solitary farmer, she would eat dense curries and fry the lining of her esophagus. She would breathe fire and light up the night—the quiet, quiet, quiet night. Never another "loaf of bread." Never another "tub of pimento cheese." She peppered her egg and ate it while writing notes, sitting on a bench in the kitchen, framing out her dumb sex story that would launch her career as a smut writer. Buy her a future peopled with animals who quietly regarded her solitude.

"MOM!" Another son galloped into the room and looked at her, with that face that means the person expects you to smile.

"Yes?"

"The puppy just bit me in the nuts!"

He grabbed his crotch comically and made an "Owwww" type expression.

"Well," she snapped, irritated by the interruption, "What do you want me to do about it?"

"Put it on the Internet," he suggested, like it was obvious. "You'll be famous in no time."

She watched him as he trotted off agreeably, to share his news with someone else, and then returned to her story.

In the woods, there was a lake so popular with boaters that the marina had clogged the water. More city folk built summer houses around the shore, and put their boats into the deep water at the marina, so the marina kept building more docks. Every year a fresh one, stained to perfection, no water marks. Between avoiding the crab pots and navigating the octopus arms of the boat docks, the boaters couldn't get their boats going fast enough to cut a rich, satisfying wake. They had to keep turning and maneuvering, so their slick white boats didn't get bogged down in the shallows. The boaters got bored, and leaving their boats permanently docked, they turned to sex for entertainment during the short mountain summer. Where before they'd skimmed the water, pulling skiers and cutting figure eights, now they hopped from deck to deck at the moorings, dipping into each other's wives, each other, and most of all into the girls who lived on the yacht at the end of the pier: The Pelican.

A fine start, she thought. *Those girls would swallow anything.* At the top of the page she wrote the title: "Sex Marina." Changed it to "Marina of Sex." She made a note in her notebook: one of the books in the series should be about a boater so sex-crazed that he puts his penis down the welcoming throat of a caught fish. When he's discovered, instead of censure, he finds his fellow fishermen curious.

Do people actually do this? she wondered.

Under the title, she wrote the pen name she'd chosen for this enterprise. Roxy Lou Reed. The name she used for writing her other books was A. C. Withers. She said because it was without a gender identifier. A man's world and all that. But really she didn't like her name: Ava. It was the kind of name you give to a baby you know will be blonde and ethereal. Ava was dark, having to bleach the hairs on her upper lip when she went out to book events. In the farm future, she would stop doing this, and let them stay black and strange. Anyway, who would put the words "Ava Withers" on the front of a book? It was like an admission of guilt.

She was fingering her lip meditatively when two of her sons came into the room, looking for beer. They didn't see her, because they were so loud, and she was all tucked away. One hoisted himself onto the counter, the other swung open the door of the fridge, retrieved two beers, and tossed one to his brother in a single graceful movement. They were athletic. They did this all the time.

"It's a Buick," said the younger one. "Sick. Suicide doors, classic street rod. I mean it's grey now…"

"So what, we make it red." The older one swung his arm expansively, waving his beer like a flag. "In the forties--"

"Wait—what are suicide doors?" she asked from the corner bench.

"Oh, sorry, mom, I didn't see you there."

The boys looked like they'd been choked.

"What are suicide doors?" She repeated.

"Sorry!" her son said. "It's just a car thing. They open backwards. A car thing!"

The boys glared at each other, shrugged, and melted away from her, back to a louder part of the apartment, taking their beers.

Suicide happens in books more than in real life, just like amnesia. Sometimes there are strange times when it happens more in the news than in real life as well. But Ava was one of those people to whom suicide happens even more frequently than in books or on TV. Both of her husbands had killed themselves. One with a gun, one with pills. She had really liked the first, loved the second. It was the second one who had fathered most of her children. What a love story they had, how sweet and tumultuous.

When she found him dead, he looked crumpled, and she hit his body. She blamed her first husband, whose death must have given him the idea. She blamed his work, very stressful and important. Most of all she blamed herself. She should have been paying more attention to the dark side of things, not trying to be so happy all the time. But there was no way to erase her mistake: it sat on her like lead. At the funeral, his mother said he was just like a hummingbird, always seemed to be hovering. She never saw that woman again after the day they buried him. Not even for the children's sake could she tolerate that nonsense. But the children didn't seem to care. All they wanted was her after all.

They tried not to talk about suicide. They knew that every little thing affected her. It was one blessed sensitivity that they could muster.

She erased the title of the short story she was writing and replaced it with "Suicide Doors." No, she thought. *That sounds like a story that no one on Amazon wants to download today.* But she couldn't let go of those words. Even after she threw a load of towels into the washer, picked up plates and glasses from in front of the television, put all the shoes by the door, she kept thinking about what suicide doors would really be. She knew her children wouldn't tell her. They got owly and weird whenever suicide came up. "Don't be morbid, mom," they would say. Her children would never be morbid. How could any group of people so physically active engage in morbidity?

She began to write again:

In the woods around the lake there are invisible doors. Suicide doors. You don't see them in the dappled shadows, between the tall trees. You don't know you're walking through one until it's too late.

"This is the reason they stay on their boats," she whispered to herself. "They all want to be out in the lake, to stay clear of the doors. But the lake gets clotted. Some people wander off."

She wrote steadily for two hours, telling the story of a girl from the yacht named The Pelican who disengaged from the watery orgy and went for a walk in the woods with Captain Rod, her paramour. One of them went through a suicide door, unaware. The other didn't know. What happened next, what happened next, and she had her story.

At noon she ate a tomato sandwich and read over her work. She printed it and took it to the girls' room, where her daughters were in towels, still wet from the showers they had taken after the morning's exercise: lacrosse, tennis, running for miles. They brushed out their long black manes, stretched their golden limbs up onto the furniture and applied their lotions, checked their toenails. She handed her pages to the middle daughter, the bookish one.

"Will you read this for me?" Ava asked.

"Oh, is this the smut?" the girl wanted to know.

"Yes," said Ava. "It's supposed to be commercial."

"Great!" and "Go mom!" the other girls chimed in. Derisive? She didn't want to know.

She wanted to believe that her girls were behind her, as their coaches said, one hundred and ten percent. They all came to her book launches, applauded her very respectable success. But they wandered off when she read her fiction out loud, became distracted by boys passing by in the street, hinged their heads down to stare at their phones, sculpted fingernails moving tentatively over the cold touch screens. Maybe if she wrote something truly accessible, her daughters would read it all the way through. Even if they laughed. Even if they were appalled. They might say, "Mom, you're such a sell-out!"

But later, in the kitchen, when she stood at the stove making salmon burgers for her children, her most bookish daughter told her, "Mom, it just isn't very sexy. It's actually kind of thoughtful."

"Really?" Ava turned, holding her spatula in front of her heart.

Her daughter tossed her graceful head. "Sorry, Mom. This is just the same old you again. I mean, it goes into a very familiar place."

Her agent, regrettably, agreed. She met him for coffee while she was waiting for her children to be done with a three hour dance class, downtown. They sat on the sidewalk, watching the passing dogs and strollers. A whiff of urine, the rind of an unidentified fruit stuck between two sidewalk blocks, a t-shirt vendor talking loudly on a cell phone, ten feet away. When the lights changed, the cars moved, buzzing, and when they changed again, the cars stopped, humming. Everyone buckled up so closely together.

Ava yearned to be away from this, the wide expanse of countryside, horses cantering in their fields, a walk in the woods. Crickets, cicadas.

"I can't write another way," said Ava.

"Can't or won't?" her agent asked, an accusation.

"I don't know?" She felt apologetic. A failure.

"Look," he told her. "Writing porn is easy—you just sit down and make shit up, let your fantasies run wild. Make a list of words: gasp, tit, fuck, cock, moan. Now use those in a sentence. Boom, you're on your way."

"I thought that's what I was doing!"

"What? 'Suicide Doors'? Does that sound like smut to you? And this girl from the boat—that's you, Ava. That's you in, like, sparkly pasties."

She finished her coffee, the sugar puddled in the bottom of the mug. She was disappointed in her inability to write even the simplest of stories without putting herself into it. How hard could it be to close that shit down for thirty thousand words? *Sex marina, marina of sex*, she thought. But those doors in the woods were invisible. How could she avoid an invisible door?

She saw her daughters ambling down the sidewalk toward her, high ponytails swinging, knocking companionably into each other, sweaty and no doubt hungry. Soon, she would be feeding them. Then, she would be washing their socks and leotards. Later, she would be writing another story. Maybe about the perverted fishermen. See if she could stop her characters from dying.

But no, the fisherman died. The inside of the fish was poison, and the story died too. Now she would try again, another character, a businessman with an ugly wife, but he loves her, he loves her. He must stay alive and out of the woods. Nothing ruins porn like mourning. She could do it, to keep him in the boats, all bumping and pushing the other boats, crowding each other in the blue lake. Why must she always be pulling at herself this way, milking a heart full of sorrow and loss? Maybe she could stop, just make some shit up. Tit, cock, groan, in order left to write. Or maybe the sound of the woodpeckers echoing through that imagined forest was just the tap of her keyboard, the beat of the hooves on the endless acres was only an echo of many human steps. She would never get away from them. Never wander off. Never experience the need to tiptoe.

As she looked out on those fields now, they were full of her children. The daughters smooth but sometimes sour, pulling up mouths of grass and glaring. The sons raucous, cantering over each other, standing up, grappling, leaving long hoof marks down each other's flanks, marks that would fill in with hair eventually and fade, inevitably, into their beautiful hides.

Airstream

Rosalynn Stovall

I want to go to the desert with you, and live
in a little sardine can trailer.

I would be established by then and you would do whatever
it is you had decided to do.
We'd eat at a road stop diner every Sunday afternoon,
And we'd only go into the city only for the essential things.

Maybe we'd have kids, raise them in the hot.
They'd be home schooled and feral. They'd grow up wise but not very
　　　smart.
I don't think we'd fight, not out there in the hot.
I don't think we'd do much of anything but be wrapped up in one
　　　another,
Living in our little sardine can, cooking in the hot.

And maybe we'd take it too far, like we are known to do.
Paint ourselves in ochre and make love.
Turn off the air conditioning and die of heat stroke.
Our bodies gray and blue, then black with putrefaction,
Festering in that trailer. Our kids playing in the sand.

TROUBLE

MR. WOLF ©A.N.S. 2/19/2013

The Canals of Mars

Lily Hoang

"I know exactly what's going to happen," he says. "You two are just going to get back together."

"He was pretty firm," Annie says. Annie says, "I don't think it's going to happen, not this time."

Thomas laughs. "You say that every time."

"But this is different, I don't know why, just that it is. It feels different."

They are children bickering as adults—am not, are too—all exchanged in social capital. They are immature, actors at professing, serious laughter at her dour circumstance.

"I'm fated to be a spinster!"

"I can't believe you," Thomas says. His face is disgusted. "You can't be a spinster, dummy. You've already been married, which means by definition, you can't be a stupid spinster, even if you wanted to be. I can't believe we're talking about this—again."

"Can you believe I used to be married?"

They are standing by a pool table. They are playing pool. Annie is no good. She only started playing because her boyfriend—her ex-boyfriend—plays. He's exceptional. Once, in one of the few romantic gestures she can remember from their relationship, Nathan looked at her, and he looked at her deeply, in a way she found wholly unrecognizable—Nathan the unaffectionate, Nathan the cold—he'd told her early in the relationship that he just wasn't an affectionate person, he didn't like to touch her, he didn't like to be touched, and Annie had accepted it, for love or something like that—and just this once, in a podunk bar, just this once he looked at her, like really looked at her, and he kept on looking at her and the pool cue struck a ball and the ball struck another but he kept on looking, right at her, right with her. They were in a small town, and he pretended he was no good at pool. He sharked townies, but not for money. Nathan doesn't need money. He's got stacks of it in bonds and stocks. He kept looking at her, their eyes finally in love for the first and only time, and the ball went in: he didn't look at the pool table, his eyes serious on hers and Annie laughed, shyly, and the moment ended. The ball rattled into the hole, but even before it did, he'd won. Now, Nathan's just about forgotten about her, and she plays pool—poorly—as remembrance, as commemoration.

"Not really," Thomas responds.

"I mean, I'm hardly an adult and already a divorcee. How unappealing: a divorcee at thirty-two."

"I think it's hot."

Annie wants her life to be like a Richard Linklater film. Instead, she waits patiently—delusionally—for Nathan to call, her phone on high right beside her, a cocked pistol.

She wants the romance of conversation and romance, but with Nathan.

Annie scans the room. She's the only Asian around, which isn't necessarily a problem, but it's also not unproblematic. "I've started seeing someone new."

"Shut up," Thomas says. "Of course you are." His face is screwed between disgust and incredulity. "Shut up, I hate you."

"Shut up, you love me," Annie raconteurs. "Get this: he's a physicist."

"Of course he is! Jesus, where do you find these guys?"

A month after Nathan broke up with her, she started an OK Cupid account. She hates using it, but she does anyways. If she had her choice, Annie would choose Nathan, and everybody knows this. "The Internet," she says.

It's seasonable outside. Inside, Annie's coat is laid in a heap. She's wearing a hexagonal shirt and striped cardigan. The patterns clash in their brightness. Thomas is wearing a plaid shirt and jeans. They are in New Mexico and it is winter. Annie still sits outside every day, writing and smoking. She used to sit outside and talk on the phone with Nathan, but now she just sits in quietude.

Thomas is no longer incredulous. "The Internet," he says, like she could do better but chooses not to.

It wasn't that long ago that Thomas was the single one and Annie had judged his Internet indiscretions. But now he's the one in a stable relationship and she's basically abandoned and too lonely.

"Sometimes, you act like such a princess," he darts.

A pool table is covered in dark blue felt. It looks oceanic and the balls are little boats holding little lives in its peril. When they crash, Annie can hear sirens. She racks.

"You know, my life is kind of like a fairy tale, you know?"

Thomas breaks. "You don't live in a fairy tale." He sinks two balls: one striped, the other solid.

"I mean, I think maybe my life is a fairy tale but it's filled to capacity with nothing but villains and I'm one of them."

The bar is full and loud.

Annie sobers her tone, says, "Did I tell you about the nightmare I had?" It's a rhetorical question and she doesn't wait for Thomas to respond. "I dreamt that I was in prison for murder. I was framed, of course, I think. I think I was framed. But I wasn't in prison yet, I was still in holding and all the other people in holding were telling me how soon, I'd be taken to the back and scrubbed down with detergent and hosed off like a protestor. I was so embarrassed for myself—isn't that ridiculous? I was embarrassed not because I'd killed somebody or was going to prison for life most likely: I cared that other people might see me naked."

"Seriously?" Thomas sinks two balls in a row. He winks; it's sweet.

"Whatever, no kicks, I don't give a fuck about dreams anyways. I mean, it's just that I woke up crying from this one. That like never happens."

People are sitting happily at their tables, sipping at their beers, boyfriends with their arms around their girlfriends. Everyone is cheerful. Annie eyes are a swarm of bright vessels, waiting for rupture.

"So I don't care about dreams, I don't invest stock in it, but whatever, my point is that I live in a stupid fairy tale."

"Stop it, you don't. I know you. You don't."

"And that's the thing, Thomas, I live in a fairy tale and my whole life is just endorsement after endorsement that this is the right way to be."

Some kids are playing shufflepuck and the machine roars. It lights up. Thomas rolls his eyes, and Annie can't tell towards whom his gesture ought be directed.

"I mean, it's like I live in this totally delusional world and everything I do contributes to furthering the delusion. Like, I'm a writer, so, strike one. For two, I'm a fucking professor, right? Students pay money to laugh at my bad jokes, and it's like, I almost buy it. But I'm not totally out of touch. I know I'm not even that funny, but the students laugh anyways because that's their role as student, and my role as professor means I can make as many corny jokes as I want and they'll indulge me, they'll make me think I'm funny when I'm not. I'm not funny at all."

He laughs and it's not malicious. It's genuine, because she's being funny, intentionally or not: she's charming.

"I mean it!" Her voice feigns offense, but she isn't really offended. She just wants to make a point. "And three: I'm a writer so I have to read, and what's more delusional than reading? I mean, reading is like the ultimate shift into delusionality."

"This is getting really ridiculous. Are you that upset about the break up?"

"Seriously? I like haven't even mentioned Nathan. You're the one bringing him up all the time."

"So you're not over him." He says this like a statement, not a question. It isn't a question at all.

"And four," Annie says, sticking four extended fingers right at Thomas's face, "I used to have a boyfriend and we'd go on these crazy adventures together and it wasn't perfect but it was fun, like really fun. So, four, now I have this fetish for long distance relationships because—go on, guess it—they're *totally delusional*." Two words become a chorused refrain, crescendos with every repetition. "I mean, what long distance relationship lasts, right? Besides, we're still in contact you know."

"Yeah, I know. You do know that you talk about Nathan, like, all the time."

"Sorry, I don't mean to. It's just, I don't know, he's different."

"Well, I'm pretty sick of hearing about him. All your friends are. Nathan this and Nathan that, and what you don't seem to understand is that you guys are in this cycle and it's boring now. You complain that he's broken up with you and then you're back in love and then it's over and repeat, Jesus."

Annie's face droops. Her eyes look ready for a rush, so she looks away. A couple in a corner booth are smitten and this only intensifies her conversation with Nathan.

"And really," Thomas says, "has anything really changed? We don't need status updates every time we see you, you know? You can talk about any number of things, but instead, you just obsess about Nathan, and honestly, I'm tired of it."

"Ok, I won't talk to you about him any more."

Offended, Thomas retaliates, "It's not just me! We all hate it!"

"Ok, I won't talk about him anymore, ok?"

"I'm just the only person who's honest enough to tell you."

"Thanks." Her voice is flat and hurt.

Tomorrow, Thomas will go to Taos and he's invited Annie along. It would be an adventure, like the ones she used to go on with Nathan. She only periodically misses him, but when she does, it is all warmth and flapping butterflies.

Annie likes Taos, even though she's never been. She really considers his offer, even though her feelings are demolished by his *honesty.*

This isn't her first invitation to Taos. Just yesterday, her old high school friend Crystal insisted she buy them a trip there. If it's something Annie hates, it's a friend who tries to buy her camaraderie, a fierce sisterhood. Crystal is everything Annie wants and despises: housewife, beautiful children, the perfect husband, wealthy. Annie's ex-husband was anything but perfect. He was—in fact—a total asshole. And Annie's life is a disaster, or, at least she thinks it's a disaster. From the outside, though, she has it all too: funny how misleading superficialities promise to be.

Annie said no to Crystal, of course, but she's never been to Taos. Two invitations in just as many days, and she wants to go, badly, just not with either of them. Nathan, however, would be the superlative choice, but he hasn't offered. He'll never offer. And Annie would rather not go at all than go without Nathan.

"I always have an escape route," Thomas says. They are at a different bar, one across the street, one that resembles an internal architecture that wants to be a martini bar but fails. "That's why we couldn't have sex," he says flatly. He's being honest again, and Annie knows this. It's not that Thomas is in love with her or anything, but she knows that if the opportunity arose, he would abandon the escape route and let desire reign.

The bartender brings out her Large Shrimp with Three Dipping Sauces. They look like frozen shrimp. They look like they were only recently thawed: barely pink and miniature. "Look at this," Annie says, her palm open against her dish. Her hand covers the smallness of the crustaceans.

"In comparison, those sauce containers look huge."

"I know, right?"

Yesterday, while Annie was on the phone with Crystal, Thomas sent her a text with a link of *Huffington Post* blog called "7 Things

You Totes Need to Stop Saying if You're Over 30." "I know, right?" stood at the dazzling second place.

Annie was still in Chicago for a reading. It was a success. The students asked smart questions and the audience was receptive, even excited. Sometimes, she has a hostile crowd, but Annie is charming and by the end, whether or not they like what she has to say, they adore her. Or, she thinks they adore her at least.

Even Crystal had praised her, in an attacking kind of way only old friends can attack: with real ammunition. The harshest criticism Thomas could propel at her would hurt less than a simple teasing joke from Crystal. There's something about nasty girlhood friendships that invite cruelty, passive-aggressive aggression. So Crystal had said, "That was really something," and Annie said, "Thanks," and Crystal said, "I can't believe they pay you for this," and Annie just stood there, and Crystal said, "I mean," and Annie said, "No kicks," and Annie said, "It's cool," and Annie said, "Let's just go get a drink," and Crystal said, "I didn't know you had all that, um, anger in you," and Annie said, "A drink?" and Crystal dug deeper, "But I liked it a lot," and Annie was like, "Really, let's just go," and Crystal said, "Remember when we were in middle school and that guy—" and Annie said, "Let's not talk about that," and Crystal said, "That's what your story reminded me of, the shooting," and Annie said, "You're saying you came to my reading and it reminded you of some psycho coming and shooting up everyone?" and Crystal said, "You were brave," and Annie said, "I was scared. I was really scared," and Crystal said, "I thought you were brave," and Annie said, "I guess you want to get your nails done tomorrow."

Annie had gone back to the hotel and she had tried not to cast Crystal as the villain. Her phone rang: the villain. "Yo," Annie said with false feminine glee, like her feelings weren't demolished, like everything was ok, and Crystal said, "Let's go somewhere together, like old times," and Annie creased her hand between the comforter and the sheets, and Crystal said, "How about Taos?" and Annie wished she was the kind of person who would know thread count, Nathan always had nice clean sheets with high thread count, her sheets were stiff and dirty, and Crystal said, "It's on me," and Annie said, "You don't need to buy my friendship," and Crystal said, "I'm not!" and Crystal said, "It's just, I want to treat you," and the sheets were soft in her fist, and Crystal said, "Let me treat you. You deserve it," and no one deserves anything, Annie doesn't believe in justice, she doesn't believe in fairness, and Annie said, "I don't need you to treat me. I can pay for myself," even though it wasn't true but Annie hated the way Crystal always made her out to be poor and struggling, like she'd been in middle school with her poor and struggling immigrant parents, and Crystal said, "I know you can," and Annie said, "I'm probably too busy with school," and Crystal said, "Please? For me? I need this. This is for me. Like, I'm really asking you."

After she hung up with Crystal, Thomas texted, "Look at #2. You say that all the time. Lol."

Annie texted back, "Ikr?" She deflated herself on the bed and looked at her phone and opened iMessage and there were no new messages, especially from Nathan.

Annie's known Crystal since forever. They're not best friends or anything, but Crystal worships Annie and her freedom and her job and her happiness, or, at least, that's how Annie makes herself out to be—against the backdrop of the perfect housewife dream that Crystal's life is.

"You know what I always hated about Nathan?" she had texted to Thomas earlier that day.

She texted quickly, before Thomas could answer, "He always texted jelly instead of jealous and I think that sounds dumb from a 32yo man. It sounds dumb unless you're a hot 20yo girl." She is a very efficient texter.

"Totes hot," Thomas had written back.

She didn't respond. She's tired of her phone. She's tired of Nathan not calling or texting or FaceTiming or anything at all. Not for days and she's sure he's moved on, *that* quickly, except he's not that kind of guy, or least she thinks he's not that kind of guy, truth is they never did get to know each other. They did drugs together and went on adventures together and they slept, cuddled up tight, together. Sleeping was their most intimate time. Together, they had fun, and fun isn't something Annie knows very much about—*tigress* Asian mother passive-aggressively pouncing, *tiger* Asian father hunting with his pack at night and never tolerating any grade below A+. "In Vietnam," he used to say, shaking his head with dismay. He never needed to finish it, Annie knew exactly what a failure she was—and they had sex, periodically, but sometimes episodically too. And then were the times it didn't work. Annie was sure it was her fault: if she were hotter, if she were a better lover. Together, they played games and she drove nine hours to see him and nine hours to go back to work, but it was worth it, she thinks, and that's what he said when he broke up with her: "It was worth it, for the good times," and it sounded cliché but they really did have some good times together and it really was worth it, to Annie at least.

If her life were a Richard Linklater film, it would be the sequel where the couple meets again. It would be the sequel to the sequel where they are fighting and still in love. She's not in love with Nathan—probably never was—not that she'd know the difference. To her, he was a symbol, a placemarker, something to show her that someone cares about her enough to respond to texts and late night phone calls. Someone to let know that her plane has safely landed. Someone to call after a job interview gone terribly wrong. Someone to call when she's offered the job anyways. And that's what Annie thinks Nathan wants too, just without the relationship anymore.

To her, he remains something of a fairy tale prince. And she is the toad, a minor character who isn't even worth a soliloquy.

Annie went on her first date with Nathan the day her sister died. She'd spent more than a week with her in Intensive Care. The doctors told her after three days in the ICU that she was going to die, that there was nothing they could do, and Annie didn't know how to tell her parents, so she didn't say anything. And then her sister died. Annie doesn't really like thinking about this though. She prefers avoiding real life, which is exactly what she was trying to communicate to Thomas.

"You want him back? Tell him about the physicist."

Annie doesn't bring him up. Thomas does—again. She knows he'll end up blaming her no matter what though, so she starts up her waxing about the lack in her life now, which isn't a big lack but it's a lack nonetheless, because they used to talk on the phone for hours every night and now those hours are free and empty. So she knits, to pass time. Does he want a scarf, she asks. But really, it's just because she bought too much yarn and needs to do something with her somnabulent hands.

Her phone buzzes. She doesn't need to tell herself it isn't Nathan, but still, she's hopeful. She flips her phone over. It's the physicist. It isn't Nathan at all.

Before there was the physicist, there was the psychologist, and before him there was the attorney—that's Nathan, who when they first met wasn't a lawyer yet but a law student and then a year passed and he graduated and he became a member of the Texas Bar and she was there for snapshots that lasted weeks. For weeks, she camped herself in his home, swinging on his hammock for hours reading *Ulysses* and writing. He wasn't used to sharing his home, but he called it *our house* and he meant it. It was *their* house, *his* house being lonely and bare without Annie there. Before the attorney, there was the painter: men caricatured by occupation. Before all those men there was the writer. Before the writer, the anarchist, whom she married. And then she wasn't married anymore. She was with the anarchist for eight years—the best years of her twenties—and she misses Nathan more than she ever missed the anarchist.

"He locked me out of his house," Annie says. "There's no way he'd care about the physicist."

"Trust me," Thomas says, "Nathan is the most predictable kind of guy. Tell him you've met someone new and he wants to take you on a trip, all of which is true, and he'll be begging you to take him back."

"I don't want him to take me back."

He makes to chock her—a gesture in gesture alone.

"I want him to love me. And then I want to reject him."

Thomas unlocks his phone and Instagrams her shrimp.

"I don't really get Instagram," Annie says.

"What? I love Instagram."

"I used to like Vine but—"

"Instagram does video now too, but you have the option of pictures. I prefer the pictures, even though I put up plenty of videos too, but pictures: they're static, and I like that."

"You're like the opposite of static, dude."

"Hey, you wanna see Seun's new haircut? It looks way sexy." He swipes at his phone, touches this and presses that. He shows her.

Thomas has been dating Seun for months now, but he doesn't call her his girlfriend even though that's basically what she is. He always calls her by her name. Annie, on the other hand, always prefaced Nathan's name with *my boyfriend*, never just Nathan, and she won't say Seun's name out of embarrassment that as an Asian, she should probably know how to correctly pronounce another Asian's name, even if they aren't the same type of Asian, even though they're nothing like sisters: there should still exist a solidarity that begins somewhere in the correct pronunciation of names.

"Don't you think her new haircut makes her look hot?"

"Yeah, she can pull off high bangs. It's hard to pull off high bangs." She refrains from saying: especially for Koreans and their fat round faces. There is such a thing as decorum, even if Thomas usually lacks it. "I bet she'd look dynamite with super short bangs, like that chick from Die Antwoord."

"But look," he says, swiping back and forth, "doesn't she look way better with this haircut?"

"They're just bangs, Thomas."

"No, it's like she just had too much hair before."

"Ok, she looks great."

"Now you're just being a bitch."

"No, I mean it. She looks great."

"Why are you always judging me?"

"What? Seriously?"

Annie removes her shrimp from its skewers. Methodically, she cuts them all in half, even though they're small enough as is, puts her knife to the side of her plate, she tries each sauce. "This is disgusting."

"Eleven dollars of disgusting."

Eleven dollars shouldn't matter to Annie, but it does. She's in her thirties—a legit adult—and she's still living paycheck to paycheck. This is the carrot, it's caught: a professor on the tenure track; she teaches mostly graduate classes; her chair has encouraged her to go up for tenure a full two years early. This is the fucking carrot, the life everyone wants, it's the cupcake and eating it too. It's every pathetic saying connected to the American dream. This is it, and somehow, being middle class is still the equivalent to being poor. Poor is maybe the wrong word: struggling is more like it. Annie isn't poor, but she feels like she is.

The irony is that she's supporting three people on her barely middle class salary, including her ex-husband, who has a trust fund but still asked her for alimony.

The day her ex-husband left, he'd walked into her office and suggested he move back to Canada to finish his PhD. She bought him a ticket within the hour. Less than twelve hours later, he boarded a one-way plane, and it was sad, even if Annie was happy—grateful—to be rid of him. His departure was tender, and she'd promised that if he needed financial support, she'd give it to him. Annie has a lot of flaws, but she keeps her promises, even if they're totally unreasonable.

"The irony," she'd said to Thomas on the phone earlier in the day, "is that I make more money than both my parents combined, and they managed a family of five and I'm somehow in debt and more fucking debt."

"It's these damn student loans." Thomas owes a lot more than Annie, but she never brings it up.

Like Thomas, Annie's late on student payments too. She's late on everything. Twice, she had her water turned off, but that was just because the city doesn't have automatic bill pay and Annie performs the role of absent-minded professor slash quirky writer to the max.

"So what do you think about Taos?"

"My friend Crystal wants me to go with her."

"But I'm talking about tomorrow. I'm going to Taos tomorrow and you can come with me."

"Why don't you ask your girlfriend?" Annie emphasizes girl-friend, elongating the consonants.

"It's a writer thing. She wouldn't want to go."

"I don't know, Thomas. I mean, here's the thing. It's just that I've been working on this book and it's going really well and I don't think I can take six hours off each way to go. That's twelve hours, and I can't spare that kind of time."

"The real irony," Thomas says, "is that if Nathan called you up, you'd be in a car going to him like it was nothing. You wouldn't even think about it."

Annie doesn't look at him. They're in a different bar and the women display scanty clothes and tanned skin.

"You don't have to go. It's fine."

"I know I don't *have* to go. It's just—I've never been to Taos."

"Then come."

"But you know how rarely we get real writing time like this and I'm so into this novel, I mean, I'm actually writing, like a lot."

"You're always writing a lot," Thomas says, jealous.

Annie is prolific. She's published a handful of books and has even more manuscripts just floating by. Thomas has two books and he hasn't finished a book since moving to New Mexico years back.

"Then don't come! Jesus, I'm not begging or anything."

"Like, I'd hate to be such a cliché, but if there's one thing I have to thank Nathan for, it's that misery is great for writing, you know?"

"Shut up. Seriously. And stop talking about Nathan. I'm sick of it, ok? All you do is waver back and forth about him. No one wants to hear about him any more. You know what we talk about when we talk about you?"

"Who?"

"All your friends, Annie. All of them. We just complain about how you obsess over Nathan. Like that's all you talk about."

"Well, he was kind of a big deal."

"You mean, he *is* kind of a big deal. Like, a really big deal."

"It really is cliché, isn't it?"

"Just stop it, ok? I don't want to hear his name ever again."

"I don't think I want to go to Taos."

"For real?"

"Yeah, I mean, I said no to Crystal. She even bought me a plane ticket. So, I mean, it wouldn't be right for me to go with you, you know?"

"I can't even believe you. This is all about Nathan, isn't it?"

Two months ago, Nathan was like, "Things just aren't working out." He'd already locked her out of his house, the same house he used to call *their* house. But Annie fought for him all the same, and then she stopped. She got in her car and was a solid hundred miles away when Nathan called and apologized, not for breaking up with her, just an apology, but he called and she turned around and drove back. She drove back and the door was unlocked.

All that Xanax they'd taken—all those drugs they did together too—does a real number on memory: theirs: when were those doors locked?: a gesture with stabbing significance to Annie.

With Nathan, she'd felt pathetic, like she was always begging for his affection, for some proof of their sentimentality, some warmth. Nathan is nothing exceptional though, not for Annie, just another among a line up of men she's been submissive to, mousy and underserving. "When are you coming here again? And where are we going? Let's go somewhere fun," she texts the physicist. She texts him, "What are you doing?"

"Getting drunk."

"Me too. With my friend Thomas." This is a lie. Annie can't drink: she tries sometimes, sipping on a drink for hours. In college, Annie used to walk around frat parties just holding a beer, and then one day, she stopped. Now she doesn't care if people judge her for not drinking, if it makes her fit in even less than she already does, if it makes her more obtrusive, as opposed to less, which is what she wants most.

It's this hypocrisy in her that she hates most—more than her obsession and sadness, her loneliness: her desire to be seen and not seen. She wants recognition and invisibility. She wants to be like you, any you, anyone who isn't Annie Tran.

He sends a wink emoticon.

She feels the cycle of inadequacy swell, insecurity.

"Is that the physicist?" Thomas asks, mid-swipe. He doesn't wait for her to answer. He shows her yet another picture on his phone. "This is from a hike Seun and I went on the other day."

"Yeah."

"Just tell me this guy is worth your time."

"Of course he is."

"Sure, just like Nathan was, right?"

Even though Thomas claims to like Nathan, Annie knows Thomas better than to believe such an obvious lie. When Nathan came to visit, they'd gone to play pool together, and both men boosted with masculinity, putting their egos at stake over a stupid game. For the record, Thomas won most of the games and any time Annie goes to visit Nathan, Thomas makes it a point to repeat that Nathan should come here instead so he can show her *boyfriend* how to play pool. He'd emphasize *boyfriend* as a slap, a reminder of how many times Nathan has broken up with her: this time is nothing new, just as Thomas had just told her—tells her now.

"What are you doing with all these men anyways, Annie?"

"He broke up with me, remember?"

"Yeah, but you don't want to be broken up."

"Yeah, but we're still broken up, it doesn't matter what I want."

Annie is rodent-like. She feels just despicable.

Annie's low self-esteem isn't a new development. She's had it since long before she knew what to call it. It's because she looked different. And she still does: look different. She can't blame all her neuroses on being Asian, but it's a big deal in that way that isn't really a big deal.

She's also never been beautiful. That's a big deal in a big deal kind of way. She's always been cute, hot even, but not beautiful, not a knockout, not gorgeous. Her sister was all of those things, but she died on the day she went out on her first date with Nathan and it's this story that she loves—the man she met on the day her sister died—not

Nathan, or, that's what Annie likes to believe anyways. Or: it's the ritual of relationships that she misses, not him. He could be anyone, although they did have some marvelous adventures together. Once, he rented a convertible and he called her into town and of course she drove eight hours to meet him and they went gambling together. The next day, they drove to Mexico. Once, they went to the Grand Canyon together and they looked from the sidelines at the big hole they never descended into. Annie had wanted to and Nathan hadn't and they didn't. Many times, they played late night Bingo. Theirs was a relationship of miniature play, macroscopic childhood, regenerated, and for Annie: the shock of fun.

Nathan, she understands, has always had fun. Their time together was not unique to her. It's because he has money. Annie grew up poor and resentful. She grew up lonely and insecure. Nathan, he grew up all those same ways but with money.

What Annie needs most—more than Nathan or fun or anything else— is another person or thing to transfer her obsession onto. Because that's what Nathan is for her: a compulsion, and she needs something else new to transport her craze onto. Into: a channel.

Her relationship with Nathan was never real anyways.

It's been nearly two years since her ex-husband left, and Annie keeps waiting for that moment when she misses him beyond pain. Two years and it hasn't happened. Of course, she spent a year and a half of that with Nathan, off mostly but when they were on, the magic.

When the Canals of Mars were first discovered in 1877, astronomer Giovanni Schiaparelli was faced with a decision: in Italian, *canali* can be translated into *canals*, which are artificial, man-made, or *channels*, which was natural, weather-made. He called them *canals*: proof of the existence of intelligent life. The canals made wild patterns along the surface of Mars, a sophisticated system—he argued—for irrigation. For decades, a telescope's precision was based on whether or not the Canals were rendered visible and distinct. The most powerful telescopes were the ones who could not only display the Canals but also their germination—their doubling, their twinning. In 1907, researchers argued that the Canals were mere illusions, but it wasn't until 1965 that NASA used photography to prove—for the first time—that the Canals did not, in fact, ever exist. Blame poor eyesight. Blame desire. Blame delusion.

Blame all you want: they were never there.

"Here's my mom's sad attempt at Christmas decorations," Thomas says, pointing at the screen. He swipes right. "And—"

Annie yawns. She tries to hide it. "Is that snowman on a fitted bed sheet?"

Thomas chuckles. "I think it's supposed to imitate snow or something."

A semi-attractive man walks past them. He's wearing a smart sweater and black plastic rimmed glasses. Annie isn't prowling, just noticing. For the last year and a half, she's chosen not to notice—for Nathan.

Nathan had never heard of polyamory before, and Annie had to explain that it was just a fancy word for an open relationship. Annie is all about fancy words, and Nathan liked it so much he tweeted it, but poly or not, neither of them ever used that trump card. They never got out of jail free—because they were never arrested in the first place. Poly was an insurance policy: because things happen: especially when they're so far apart: living their lives: separately.

Annie smothers a laugh. Thomas starts talking again. He's under the impression that Annie is actually enjoying this picture tour through his phone, but really, she's laughing at a memory: a few months ago, she's in Houston with Nathan, and they're talking about Twitter, and she says something about how long it took her to realize that his handle—@growler303—was in reference to a growler of beer, which he drinks in excess, and he says no, it's because he's like a kitty and growls, which doesn't even make sense, but it was endearing. Then, he said something about how her Twitter handle—@camerainsecura—was all about how she's insecure around cameras. He didn't even get the pun.

"And here's me with my mom."

Annie makes a sound to placate him beyond her boredom. She hopes he'll stop, but she knows Thomas well enough to know that he could go on for hours like this. Once he starts, the end is never inevitable.

"There's free wifi here, so this isn't even on my data. Hold on, look at this one." He keeps swiping, cropped bodies and limbs flurry the screen, corybantic.

"Hey, dummy, look at your phone. Don't you know what the wireless icon looks like? You're not even on the wifi here."

"Oh," Thomas says, in an obvious attempt to make it seem like he cares what she's saying, "check it out. I got this cool app that tells you how much data you've used."

"I've got unlimited data."

"Fuck, you must've been grandfathered in."

Another quasi-handsome man walks in. Annie looks briefly but finds herself suddenly fatigued: with the conversation, with her life, with the fixed idea of romance.

"You know what Nathan said?" Annie's voice is at once resigned and furious.

"Jesus—"

"He said I'm unstable. Me! Like he's got any room to—"

"Umm—"

"He says I'm unstable, that I take too many pills, and then, before I leave, he's got the nerve to ask me for a stock supply of Xanax. And this is *after* he's dumped me! I mean, he's the fucking alcoholic!"

"You know, he's right, Annie."

"What?"

"You *are* a little unstable."

Appalled, she says, "You think I'm unstable."

"Yeah, you're like the most unstable person I know."

Erasure starts playing. Annie loves Erasure.

"Hey, let's go karaoke." Thomas ganders that he's hurt her feelings, which he has, and she knows immediately the trick he's trying to play.

"I hate karaoke."

"But you're Asian! Isn't that like a requirement or something?"

"My mom used to have a machine," but the truth is that Annie doesn't like to do anything she isn't immediately good at—except pool, but that just for the sake of sentiment and an attempt to rejuvenate a memory that's already waning.

Her phone buzzes. *It's not Nathan*, she tells herself.

It isn't Nathan. It's the physicist. "That was blissful," he texts, in reference to the weekend they just spent together.

"Yes," she responds. "It was."

"I appreciate you," he texts back.

"How about bowling?" Thomas asks.

"It's getting late. It'll be closed, and besides, bowling's no fun with just two people." Nathan and Annie used to go bowling all the time, just the two of them. Sometimes, he invited friends along, but every time, it was fun.

Later that night, Annie will be the one scrolling through pictures on her phone. She has no one to show them to though. She stops at one, one that Nathan had texted to her a month ago. It's the two of them at a Greek festival they just happened to walk by. She'd convinced him it would be fun. Inside, he bought some art. She bought a baklava sundae, which they shared, with one spoon. It was a tender moment.

Nathan is a full foot taller than her.

He's standing, with good posture.

He has his arm around her.

She is looking at him.

They both look stern. An old Greek man had shot the picture. Accompanying the photograph, Nathan had texted, "Why so stern?"

Annie plugs in her phone, sets it to silent, and sleeps with panic and hope.

Perseveration

Dana Koster

Reclusive and necrotic I troubled the woodpile
    logs that seemed to stack themselves
        left me blistered
      tore themselves down

I have made life
inside me once before
    death too
          have spun
          my disorderly threads
watched them knit themselves
      into sweaters
   into knots
     into arms
so pale and long
      I could tie them in a bow

the logs
        troubled me
the logs seemed stacked
        against us
against the house

                  life's leaded dust

escaped through cracks

                      in the plaster

we have become

               the house stacking

and unstacking itself

by the end

I needed an end

            I could have burned it all

      to the ground

The wind blew cool that night down the mountain slope. auntie Chris started a fire in the big-mouthed, black-mouthed place. Rob was eager to interest Farmer Gray in the subject of bears, wolves, and her specimens of wild game, and as Ralph and Rick cordially conded

Rob, the farmer told his younger days, when such gentle creature a Bruin could be occasional seen Then L added:

"As have said, bears could be seen far of er than now, and yet I think I have seen bear tracks in my fields within a few days."

"Within a few days?" asked Rob erly.

think so," rmer.

ee of the boys leaned intently f ing, in the depths of their s

ncle Nat, "bears won

How We Grieve

JJ Chen Henderson

an internal dialogue between daughter and mother

Your feet are swollen and grey,
as if they are two doves stranded in snow.

    Your feet shuffle,
    as if you are pulling the house behind you.

The beat-up respirator on your nose
makes you look like an old elephant.

    Your nose is running into your mouth—
    you always did like to eat boogers as a child.

Your skin has become a crumpled map;
I can only recognize your bones.

    You are jumping out of yours—
    that's not how you molt.

Why the shaky hands, then?
Is my photo album that heavy? Wimp.

Why the wobbly knees?
Are you carrying stones in your pockets? Wimp yourself.

You are so Goddamn fast
the gate will bounce you right back. I swear.

Take your time,
please. Promise.

MTV Poem #10
Paula Abdul, *Rush, Rush*

Daniel Romo

Countdown to Keanu in 3… 2… 1… Who isn't smitten with an exotic schoolgirl decked in a ponytail, bustier, and pencil skirt? But she has a boyfriend and not even a pre-*Matrix* squint or coy smile can pry her away. Paula does what Paula does best and dances around as if the viewer gets two videos in one. Spandex and fur bras are the recommended ensemble when dealing with deep feelings. Field trip to the observatory: Keanu mocks his competition because he knows they are nobodies and sees his reflection in the stars. But they get even, and stabbing a man's whitewalls is fightin' words…RACETIME! Keanu and his rival drag down the dirt because the street would be too easy. Who can stay in the car the longest before the earth below becomes a memorial. How simple it is to lose sight of an oncoming ledge in the name of ego and love. Keanu has always been a sad man, but apparently, rubbing a glass jug of milk against your face helps one forget death. But I can attest to the fact that getting drunk for the first time sophomore year can't lessen the effect of loneliness. The violins play while Paula pours her heart out and Keanu spits out cheese masked as words. This helps console her over her bf's death and she and Keanu blow out the candles and kiss in an abandoned mansion as if the evaporating smoke has always been hotter than the flame.

excerpt from Lobe

Jay Ponteri

I bore people. I'm too ironic. This morning for breakfast I'm drinking a 12-ounce latte and eating a bacon-and-egg sandwich. I probably won't eat anything else till dinner or right before dinner. I might snack on chips and bean dip. If I had some cash to throw at a project, I'd publish David Markson's last four books in a single, beautifully designed hardcovered edition and give copies away to anybody who wanted one. I try to practice kindness. I do and say things. I move my toes and fingers. All shook down. Do not confuse kindness with cheerfulness. One of my kind acts today was listening to my friend, to try to understand what it was she was saying, so she could see herself being seen by another. Another was helping a man sitting next to me who was having a coughing fit. I'm trained in First Aid and CPR. I need to renew my certifications. An act of kindness is a brave act of constructing the self in relation to The Other. It's reaching out and reaching in at the same time. Kindness pushes back against the forces of decay, destruction, and death. I try to avoid conflict. If you're not giving me what I need I may not say a thing. I may not tell you I disagree with you even though I do. I make promises I cannot keep. I over-include, I over-indulge. I say yes more than I say no. I'll give you a ride to Eureka and not charge you for gas. Eureka seems to me a little tired, a little fried. I'll buy your lunch if I have enough money in my account to cover it. I could live there. I'll recommend you when I shouldn't. I'm a people pleaser and I do and don't like that about my-self. I may do more for you than you do for me unless you are my wife whose generosity I cannot begin to match, whom too often I neglect or push away. I could give more of myself to my wife but choose otherwise. By otherwise, I mean What I want. I'll do your dirty dishes. I'll do you. I'm coming to understand practicing kindness involves not only empathy and reaching out towards others and the self at the same time but honesty and direct expression. Kindness is about shedding the ego, about serving The Other while forgetting and not forgetting the self. Doing something for somebody not because you want something from them in return, not because you secretly love them or want to fuck them. Last night my leg fell asleep. Last night I felt nostalgic for a fantasy I once cultivated. I didn't fantasize—I remembered a fantasy. I don't like cheerful people. Cheerful people have some difficult work ahead of them and I can't help. I don't mind staring at a blank page. My favorite writers have all stared at blank pages. Robert Walser stared at a blank page. Mary Ruefle has stared at a blank page. Dad used to kick the tires as a way of assuring himself his car functioned properly. I love Dad. I love Mom. I don't call them enough. My plan is to stand by their respective death beds. I like making funny faces at newborn babies. I have read *Paradise Lost* and *Paradise Regained* by John Milton. I used to buy a lot of records and CDs and see bands but now I buy a lot of books and attend readings. I listen to music privately, through headphones or in my Honda. My subwoofer is located in the trunk of my Honda. My beating heart is located on the left side of my chest. My soul is located in an alley off West Kilbourn Avenue in Milwaukee, Wisconsin. The numeric combination to the lock on my 8th grade locker is located in The Abyss. My former lovers are located outside of The Abyss. Charlotte is located in North Carolina. The hospital at which I was born prematurely is located in Charlotte. Mom is located in Mishawaka, dad in Oak Brook, Illinois. Only 100 or so miles separate Oak Brook from Mishawaka. Two very distinct ways of life separate Oak Brook from Mishawaka. Whereas Oak Brook is elegantly, precisely catered, smoothly pressed and polished, Mishawaka is that old neighborhood tavern that has a separate area for family dining off the bar. Oak Brook is reaching for something—Mishawaka is what it is. I don't drink much alcohol, maybe one beer or glass of wine per month. I smoke weed like three to four times a month, often less than that. I buy three to four books per week, sometimes more. My first girlfriend was Karen XXXX. In 6th grade Karen and I kissed at Camp Eberhart. It was my first kiss and I hope it was hers. On the bus ride back to Mishawaka we sat together and held hands and I remember her saying to me, her voice joyfully anxious, that she'd never held hands so much in her life. When she broke up with me in 7th grade, I cried. I'm a tiger standing in the corner pouncing on nothing.

A FUTURE OF TYRRANY AND OPPRESSION

MR.WOLF©ARONNELSSTEINKE.COM 5/25/2014

Pots

Kim Chinquee

On my street, I watch the houses grow like plants. The roofs and sidings, stone. Structures. There are twenty-four, and I'm told there will be more, once the politics are worked through.

I bought the last lot available. The day after I put down my deposit, my then-boyfriend and I broke up because I said I'd never let him move there. I have legs of my own that don't knock me over.

When my house was done, the builders gave me the keys and said to me, It's yours now. The next day the movers brought the stuff from my apartment, and I had my new fridge and stove delivered. Washer, dryer, and then came my new yellow chair, teal couch, and then, made by a local artist, came my kitchen table. I'd had my desk refurbished and that came that day too. The desk was a gift from a former colleague, something she'd acquired from another professor who literally died with his head there.

Most nights I fall asleep there, working on my research about the stamina of bees. Last night, I awoke curled in my desk chair.

I bought these potted plants to put on my step mostly because I don't have a lawn yet.

When my neighbors are away I go next door and prune. I water. I sit on their back patio with the umbrella folded, talking to my friend Jan. When I lived in my apartment and she lived in hers, we lived across the street from each other. Then she moved. One night she called to tell me that during rounds with her residents (she's a trauma surgeon), they decided to admit her to the ER, thinking she was stroking. Maybe diabetic. They said she made no sense. Until they tested.

When she called from rehab, she said, This is me. This is who I am now.

My plants want water every day. I don't even know what to call them.

I also have herb plants in my windows. I also have an orchid plant that never seems to change. I feed it ice cubes, like the directions tell me, to the sides of it.

The Road to Hibbing
[Busking at Bob's]

Rafael Alvarez

"*So, you get the third concept—these two things don't belong together but somebody put them there...you get the extra message...*"

—Frank Zappa

Some are dusted lightly, the glint compounded for years in a pestle of
Fortuna and hard work to achieve modest success and the occasional,
longed-for turn among the stars.

This is Basilio.

Others—like the sculptor Hettleman with whom Basilio haunt-
ed the ruined streets of Baltimore—are born with the gift in full; the
charge stronger than the filament into which it descends. They seldom
live beyond 30 without languishing on locked wards and cell blocks,
using toothpicks to make tapestries of Calvary from unraveled socks.

And then there is India, who received the spark in spades and
does the work; kin to once-in-a-lifetime prodigies forced to tell the
world to back off, that the gift was given to them. From birth she has
had the poles of Basilio and Hettleman before her.

Struggle and surrender; failure as prologue and failure as fate,
solubles and sobriety.

"You're taking her where?" asked Hettleman the night before
Basilio shoved off from Crabtown.

"Clear Lake," said Basilio.

"She likes to fish?"

"A cornfield—Iowa."

"Where every kid wants to go," said Hettleman, handing Basilio his old Boy Scout sleeping bag that the young musician would use every night for the next thirteen weeks.

We find father and daughter about to depart the Great Magnolia State a month before India's 12th birthday, touring the lower 48 in a Chevrolet station wagon during the Great Rock & Roll Road Trip.

The adventure took them from Baltimore to the Badlands and back—Memorial Day to Labor Day—up, down and across the Continent as Basilio painted the history of American music at the longitudes and latitudes where it had descended into upright pianos and busted guitars in the wake of the Korean War.

In the evenings, after long afternoons at public swimming pools where he sketched in a composition book and snoozed beneath an orange floppy hat while India swam, Basilio set up his easel at campgrounds.

The night before, in Tupelo, he set aside a stretched and gessoed canvas intended for a still life of a voluptuous fig tree (from a Hettleman photograph: "*I'm swinging over like a heavy loaded fruit tree...*") at 2019 Whittier Avenue in West Baltimore; postponed it to paint the face of the King on the reverse of a wheat penny with a brush made from a single strand of horsehair.

Render unto...

Named for the sub-continent of color—as tanned and smooth as a hazelnut in a pink Elvis t-shirt from the gift shop—India practiced the violin at the other end of the picnic table, the scents of *grandiflora* and turpentine mixing in the afternoon light over Tombigbee State Park.

A thousand miles away, the girl's mother wondered what the god-forsaken cotton fields of Mississippi had to do with an adolescent girl's summer vacation.

Standard exercises, a few songs of her own choosing for fun—, arrangements harder than she could handle; a sip of grape juice with each turned page.

"How much more, Dad?"

The answer was always the same: "Twenty minutes."

"Give it another twenty," he said, working the penny with a magnifying glass, "and I'll make us some sandwiches."

She always complied (for her, not for him, something Basilio wouldn't realize for years), sawing through Shostakovich as Basilio chopped pickles from the ice chest for tuna salad mixed with gas station packets of mayo. They drank cold water from the melted ice and shared a Hershey's with almonds for dessert before twilight games of chess and reading by flashlight in the tent.

Goodnight, say your prayers, we'll call Mom from the road in the morning.

Living together for the first time since the divorce, they learned to get along as only a couple of hard-heads trapped for thousands of miles in a moving vehicle are able.

Contentiously inane debates about the difference between reading a map and reading music.

Agreement that better music is often found in Nowhereseville, USA on the AM instead of the FM.

And, if you sleep in a beat-up station wagon with out-of-state plates and provocative bumper stickers—EAT BERTHA'S MUSSELS

—behind a Protestant church Deep in the Heart of Dixie, you will en-
counter the drawn gun and hard questions of a skeptical sheriff before
the cock crows.

Is this child your daughter?

[Yes.]

Is this man your father?

[Yes sir.]

Why did you choose to park here?

[It seemed safe.]

May I search your vehicle?

[Yes.]

What are all these paintbrushes?

[I'm a painter.]

Can you prove this child is your daughter?

[Fold and spindle: a copy of India's birth certificate from a yel-
lowed envelope that Trudy insisted he bring along.]

Boss Man left with the finest of the wheat pennies—Lou-
isiana Hayride Elvis, touched up that morning—and a parting
word.

"Churches get broken into all the time, even in Mayberry. If
you need to sleep in the car, pull into a nice hotel somewhere and park
between the other vehicles. No one will bother you and you can go in
and use the bathrooms in the morning. Grab a free coffee and some
corn flakes for the kid."

Basilio hit the highway immediately, west along the top of Mississippi as India slept; dawn breaking over the Father of All Waters as
they crossed the Memphis/Arkansas Bridge on Highway 61 of lament
and lore: Polly Jean by way of Bob as bequeathed by an earlier, more
nimble Robert of darker hubris.

The rising sun on India's side of the car struck the curve of her forehead in a way that reminded Basilio of his father and, moved by this, he touched her hair. Half asleep, she stirred and asked what would have happened.

"What do you mean?"

"If he didn't believe I was your daughter?"

They were in West Memphis now—Arkansas—headed for St. Louis where Basilio knew an Italian guy from his grandparents' neighborhood who would make them lunch. He pulled into a gas station for coffee and on the way back leaned in the passenger window to give India a bottle of orange juice.

Flipping down the visor in front of her, he angled the cracked mirror so it filled with her dark eyes, brown hair, round cheeks.

"Look."

"Yes?"

"No one will ever believe that you are not my daughter."

Fourteen hours, two fill-ups, a bag of cheeseburgers, half-a-milkshake each, a dozen homemade Italian cookies from Genovese and 820 miles later, Basilio slipped the wagon between other vehicles-on-vacation at a Best Western in the Land of 10,000 Lakes, dazed from the road and one tank of gas away from broke.

He could call his father (he could always call his father, anytime from anywhere) but it didn't feel like an emergency. He could call Trudy, but—a thousand miles from home with nothing in his pockets but Elvis Presley pennies—that would make it an emergency.

And all Hettleman had to spare was the sleeping bag.

"Sit tight," he said to India as she shimmied into the bag in the back of the wagon with the last of the St. Louis cookies and her mother's college copy of Karamazov which, like the Shostakovich, was far enough beyond the child's understanding to hold her interest.

From a payphone at a gas station next to the motel, he called Miss Bonnie, a barmaid he trusted like a grandmother who functioned as his agent. It was just past 11 p.m. in Crabtown and the bar sounded dead on the other end of the line.

At Bonnie's, he'd left a pair of quick-sale paintings—Baltimore Coal Pier, 1957 and Sunrise Over the Bottle Cap Factory—a steal at $200 each.

"Sorry darling, things are slow. Only the rum-pots been coming around. You okay?"

"Yep. Just checking."

"How's my girl?"

"Having the time of her life."

"Some folks been asking about the Grandpop pictures. Ain't from around here. Wanna see if I can sell one of those?"

"No, no, take those down" said Basilio quickly. "I'll call you later."

"Suit yourself."

Pumping gas the next morning—topping the tank with three bucks and some change left over; not a grain of oatmeal to mix with warm water from the wash room spigot—Basilio watched his daughter brush her teeth in the passenger seat.

She swished water round in her mouth, opened the door to spit on the ground and spied her father at the rear of the car.

"Morning, Dad."

"Morning, hon."

Through the wagon's long windows he watched her dig out an almost-empty jar of peanut butter and pop open a can of garbanzo beans. She jiggled a dozen or so chick peas into the peanut butter and, with a Popsicle stick from the day before, mixed them in the jar.

Les haricots avec sauce aux cacahuètes.

Basilio returned the nozzle to the pump and moved forward half-a-foot for a better view. Diligent and contented—riding some *brio* far beyond the dirty hood of a station wagon in Minneapolis—India balanced a single glazed bean on the end of the stick and brought it to her mouth.

Cranium shaped garbanzos (Basilio knew folks back home with heads shaped like chick peas, several ran their mouths over 75-cent drafts at Bonnie's) slathered with peanut butter and eaten from the end of a stick; a balancing act, a game.

Basilio knew (just as India knew they were down to beans and nickels, thrilled with an errant quarter buried beneath cassette tapes) that if she hadn't found the ice cream stick she would have used a twig or a pencil—whatever worked.

And in that moment, wiping his hands on a paper towel as he came to the driver's side, he sensed something in the girl that his prejudice kept him from seeing in her mother. It was a part of himself—his most valued trait, a near-reckless surety that came with the sparkle —that Trudy (and those before her, those during her, those after her) found attractive until it wasn't.

Knowing it was hard-wired into his daughter, as it had in Basilio's grandfather for whom he'd been named, gave him an idea on how to invest this last tank of gas.

["YOU PIMPED OUR DAUGTHER ON THE STREET?

"I was teaching her to work."

"SHE'S TWELVE YEARS OLD."

"It beats taking out the trash and doing the dishes for allow-ance."]

He turned the ignition and pulled away from the station, India not paying attention until Polly Jean came out of the dash and Bobby Z went in: "*…where the winds hit heavy…*"

With the skyline of Coon Rapids before them, he let the song play through once and hit rewind.

Anoka and Sandstone, red iron pits running empty.

"Can you learn this by tomorrow morning?"

India's finger on the rewind: Cloquet en route to 2410 Seventh Avenue East.

Once more with feeling, empty can of beans at her feet as she chewed the flat wooden stick.

"I know it now."

Instinct

Wendy C. Ortiz

The sliding glass door opens and we begin the descent into the weekend. My new Scholastic Books order arrives and eager to read I prepare the fortress of blankets, small tables serving as a roof, the flashlight my little lighthouse. The two of them help me and I begin to see the trickery. The moment a child can see when the parents want to be rid of them even for just a little while the child can see through herself in the mirrored walls and the fort becomes a hovel of loss. The swamp cooler kicks in and the TV as always is on. The voices disappear down the hallway. A door closes. The cartoons are long over. Open season on the TV screen for little girls whose eyes and ears are developing the instinct. The clear liquid, the Popov, is drained from its bottle. The instinct is for danger. The moss green carpet is a bed. The instinct develops beneath the skin. I don't yet know that in this battle I will develop the necessary scar tissue. For now I must defend the fort, claim it as my own. The instinct, then, begins deep in the young nerves. The fort makes it own walls, foundation. The fort's walls cement over with knowing.

The 99 Revolutions

Nick Triolo

It's Friday night, I'm ejected from work, and I suffer from a case of the "DigiEye." After a ten-hour staring contest with my laptop, I'm convinced that machines can make eyes bleed. I spill out onto the streets of downtown Portland, Oregon, and peer back at my 34-story office building, a stack of brick and steel. Feeling disoriented, I scramble to remember—to feel again, to inhabit—this outside world.

I told myself I wouldn't do this.

I told myself I wouldn't box in my life.

I told myself to defy the cubicle trap, to slash with a hatchet any beige-colored office partition that got in my way. But it got me. A nonprofit intercultural organization had created a position just for me and I couldn't resist. They were doing important work and I was desperate for stability, anything to keep me in one place and doing something good, something generative. So, I said yes to the beige.

Pale streetlights expose the filthy bus terminal nearest my office. Its stench of urine—composed more of whiskey than water—alchemizes with perfume trailing a businesswoman in stilettos click-clacking behind me, on pace for a Nordstrom's Christmas sale. My bus approaches and I step on with a few others. An elderly man dressed entirely in brown snores to my left, using crumpled newspaper for a pillow. In front of me, a red seat has a sticker on it. The image is a circular snake with one word in Soviet-era block print: "STRIKE!"

It is December of 2011 and Occupy Wall Street has just been beaten down to a definitive pulp. Remnants of this cultural rupture still sweep through Portland streets. For me, Occupy was as much a revolution of my self as it was a global shift. Before, I wasn't a committed activist and didn't have many friends who were. I remember, before attending my first General Assembly, having to look up the word "subversive." And yet, after hearing this worldwide wakeup call, I began to attend affinity group meetings, helped plan marches, and organized banner drops. I could no longer go back to sleep.

Entering my apartment, I hold anxiety in my clavicle and need to be outside, not bound to another box. I need to move, to cut through wind and shuck off the day's sludge. Demands are simple: Outside. Solitude. Movement.

So, I decide to go for a run.

Chapman Square sleeps. For forty days, these three city blocks served as a settlement for urban miners to pan the muddied creeks of capitalism for truth. As the biggest Occupy camp outside Wall Street, this site became a collective brainstorm of ideas, food sharing, and education. On November 13th, 2011, riot police arrived, looking prepared for chemical warfare. Tens of thousands of citizens came to resist the camp's takeover, which proved successful for a few days. But shortly after, hundreds more police arrived and quickly reduced the camp to rubble.

I haven't returned to Chapman Square since the eviction, and I wonder what it looks like now. I cinch my hood tight and pin an orange patch to my sleeve, which has an image of a clenched fist on it, the one I wore for every rally. I blend into the night and travel towards the city lights. Downtown Portland is buzzing. Young urbanites swarm bars with cheap beer and pizza grease to decompress from a stressful week. As I approach Chapman Square, I notice high fences placed around its perimeter, so I decide to run one lap around the square. I pass two police officers in orange jackets guarding the park by walking its perimeter.

"Passing on your left," I announce, approaching them from behind. No response.

Peering through the chain-link fortress, my mind strolls through the communal kitchen that once was, into the People's Library where workshops happened. I float above memories of the hundreds of tents and tarps, crazy eyes squinting, animated conversations. My nostrils recall filth and mud and panhandling parades of grime. And the rats. I never slept a night at the camp, but I still find myself homesick for such a raw gathering-place.

As I run around the three blocks, I pass an older couple strolling to their vehicle after a holiday performance at Shnitzer Hall. They hold each other close as the warmth of the hall escapes from their wool coats. I wonder how these elderly view the state of things today, and what their hearts have already navigated— the Great Depression, World War, Nazis, nuclear deployment, the Vietnam War, Khmer Rouge, Korea, the civil rights and environmental movements. Two minutes later and a full lap around Chapman Square, I begin a second. Then another. Then another. I wonder how 99 laps might feel tonight, to pay a private tribute to the 99%, those around the world who are paying the price for the destructive forces of a small, global elite.

The laps continue.

Lap 10

I find this urban lap to be uninspiring, but I can't seem to stop. Moving repetitively around a quarter-mile rectangle of unforgiving cement is less demanding on the body than on the mind. And yet there is still something special about propelling forward simply for the sake of moving. I think of Sri Chimnoy's 10-day transcendent foot races, Satish Kumar's 34,000-mile walk protesting nuclear proliferation, and Native American transcontinental walks. As I settle into an unexpected orbit around Chapman Square, I begin to understand the magic in the monotony.

To remember my number of laps, I pair each circuit with the corresponding year of my life. On lap twelve, I review age twelve—my family moved to the Sierra Nevada foothills, I won a skate competition, and what little I knew of my government, I trusted. After reaching my current age of 27, I imagine on each following lap what these future years might look like for me, for the planet. On the thirty-third circuit, I stop, reverse my direction and start running and counting again.

Lap 35

I have to pee. I take this opportunity to visit the candlelight vigil at City Hall across the street and ask the protestors where they relieve themselves. This vigil is the last flame remaining from the occupation, and I find it rather depressing: an old man sits shivering and silent, waiting patiently for change, while five street kids—dogs, bandanas and face tattoos—lean on their canvas backpacks and smoke hand-rolled cigarettes.

"Any of you know of a public bathroom around here?" I ask.

"Yah, there's one in the parking garage," the larger one responds. "Probably closed though. Honestly, I would just whip 'er out in them bushes right there." His greasy index finger points towards a cluster of bushes across the street. The kid retreats behind glasses, resting his head on the dog's flank.

I strike up conversation with the others and mention my idea of circling Chapman Square 99 times. They are hardly intrigued. Minutes later, as though my words had to first ricochet off nearby buildings to reach their ears, one guy responds:

"99 laps? Shit, I may be able to run 99 feet!" The boys laugh and cough and twitch nervously. The old man doesn't move a muscle. After sharing some stories, the group wishes me luck and promises to call 9-1-1 if they look over and see me on the pavement crawling. I thank them for their crude blessings and cross the road to urinate on the dying urban flora.

Lap 52

After two hours of circling city blocks, I watch as fog infiltrates the city and cloaks surrounding skyscrapers. Moisture joins a green light on top of the Wells Fargo Building to create a severe laser beam that slices through the night, an authoritative eye scanning its subjects.

The two policemen return to their guard post after a break, and this time I'm running straight towards them. I catch one officer taking a discerning glance at me. *Finally*, I think to myself. It's only taken fifty laps to get some attention. Excited by the opportunity for dialogue, I begin to formulate a response to their interrogation, but after passing three more times over the next several minutes, I realize they still have no interest in me.

I, however, develop a keen interest in them. In each passing, I tap into their conversations, which are dominated by two topics: girls and music. One of the guards holds his head up to an iPhone blaring gangster rap. As I pass them a dozen more times, I learn that the other officer is experiencing sexual challenges with his "manic" girlfriend, Trinity. Despite our different trajectories, the three of us venture through this December night together, inhabiting some shared state of monotony and inquiry.

Lap 66

It's past midnight and my legs feel heavy from the repetitive pounding. Policemen filter out of Central Precinct for their night shifts, shotguns and riot gear dangling. The police are not the problem, I realize. They too are good-natured humans, full of veins and brains, blood and guts. They too have families. They too carry around histories of abuse, high cholesterol, car payments, and subprime mortgages. They too could be full of love or empty of it entirely. And they too are part of the 99%. Returning to breath, I continue.

Lap 80

I'm tired of this shit, this cold, boring loop. I want to go home. I wonder why I even decided to do this in the first place. Who cares? No one. Nothing changes because of this. I take inventory of my reasons for being here, and I'm reminded of the discomfort during any major transformation—traveling from womb to world; growing pains; confronting an enemy; moving past old relationships; quitting a job to pursue a passion; accepting death; waking up to a system that's required your submission and saying: "Nope. No way. Not anymore." There's an endurance that's necessary in the struggle for social and environmental equity, to trudge forth through swamps of defeat. I gather this kindling and set it ablaze, regaining control of my smoldering fire still burning inside.

Lap 99

Deep into the fourth hour, I reach the 99th lap and imagine something tripping me, or a police officer coming to foil my plan on the last revolution. Nothing so dramatic unfolds as I take the four familiar lefts and return to my starting point.

Then I stop moving.

With little hesitation, I find myself running yet again, hobbling but destined to complete one final loop. I finally understand that no one is left out of this ecological endgame. No one can escape the challenges our planet faces. Whether I like it or not, I'm in this together, together with greedy CEOs and child sex offenders. I'm in this together with lovers and loathers, bodhisattvas and border patrol. I'm in this together with devastating earthquakes and radiant sunsets, great blue herons and barrel-bodied armadillos. To think of my mind and my heart as separate from anyone and everything is perhaps my biggest failure, my greatest illusion. And to revolve around something as innocuous as three city blocks brings forth something deeper, some dimension of revolution inherent in everything. Even as our planet orbits the Sun, each day it takes on a different, more complex form. If we're all in this together, then it must be true that such centrifugal force reflects within us a shared cycle of growth, of transformation, and of unavoidable, inescapable *revolution.*

Surrendering to this thought, the last lap feels like the first.

I HAVE MADE AN IMPRESSION

MR. WOLF © A.N.S. 11/11/2014 ARONNELSSTEINKE.COM

Family History

Dana Koster

The nights he didn't sleep and didn't need to
my brother picked electronics to bits: removed microphones
from the bag-end of the vacuum cleaner. Blared Zappa,
hosed shattered hard drives off a second story porch.
But who could be satisfied with the apartment stripped clean
of its monitoring equipment? Who wouldn't wander by day
the rails that slunk through strawberry fields, or itch
to lay a nickel on the tracks, leave your hand there?
Watch it emerge a new object. Flattened by the train,
blurred of its distinctions.

Cabo San Lucas

Steve Denniston

My grandfather's wife became sick and they told me it was cancer. Dad told me not to expect a miracle. I was old enough to understand it wasn't fair, but not old enough that I knew how to say it. All my dad said was, the poor bastard. It was the second time Grandfather took a wife to the doctor for that diagnosis.

Hospital visits were short and polite. I knew what to expect, having been through it with my first grandma. Of course, so did Grandfather.

With his second wife, a few months into the cancer, he started buying things like flax seed oil for her. And cod liver oil, glutamine, green tea, lots of food with phytochemicals, then only gluten free food. His house had huge bottles of vitamin A, zinc, and vitamin B. He never bought any of that when his first wife was sick.

What the hell is phytochemicals, my dad asked. Grandfather gave him an article to read.

And cod liver oil? And why green tea? There were articles for those things too.

Can you believe this, my dad said to me, it's beginning to sound desperate.

She died in Mexico. Grandfather took her there to try a therapy that couldn't be done in the United States. My dad said she was dead before they left, so why'd they bother going. Even back then I wondered which town they went to in Mexico. I wanted to ask Grandfather after the funeral but my dad told me to leave him alone, he was mourning.

My son wakes me up. It's early, but not early enough it's worth going back to sleep. "The dog slobbered on my blanket again," he says. "A big wet spot under his mouth." These days that's one of the funnier things in my son's life. The fact that dogs slobber in their sleep.

"Did you let him out?" I say.

"No, he was sleeping."

I sit up, put my feet on the floor. "Let's go to the kitchen, I'm thirsty."

He covers his mouth and nose with his pajama top. "You have stinky dog breath."

My wife pretends she's asleep. I close the door quietly.

His pajamas are colored like a panda. We bought them at the end of last winter. When we pulled them out this winter they still fit him. They should be too small, or at least too short.

We go into the kitchen and I drink two glasses of water with some Tylenol to help my headache. The dog is at the back door waiting and I let her out. I can't tell if my son sleeps any better with the dog on his bed, but he thinks he does. I want to believe he does.

"What do you want for breakfast?" I ask.

"I'm not hungry." The short, quick, cranky voice. He is tired of this argument too. Last night I fixed chicken strips and tater tots for dinner, his favorite. He ate one tater tot.

"How about a milkshake?" I say. Anything to get a few calories in him.

He stops playing with the fridge magnets. "For breakfast?"

We dump whole milk and ice into the blender. And a banana, fuji apple, honey, two kiwi, a Flintstone vitamin which makes him smile, some strawberries, and Sunny Delight. The glasses we will use are already on the counter. His glass has Tri-Zyme in it, two pills I ground up the night before.

I didn't tell his doctor I was trying the enzyme. All the doctor does is prescribe medicines that make my son sick in different ways. It's depressing, reading all the side effects and then waiting for them to manifest.

The enzymes aren't prescription. Or over the counter. I mailed an order to the company, out of the country. It was very old fashioned, a money order in the mail instead of a credit card over the internet.

"That's not a milkshake," my son says. "Where's the ice cream?"

"It's a tropical milkshake."

He pushes the puree button and we can't talk because it's so loud. The fruit moves into the blades and the pitch of the blender drops to a low growl. I fill our glasses and stir his to mix the enzyme.

"This is how they make them in Cabo San Lucas," I say. "It's too warm for ice cream there."

"Where's that?" he asks.

"Far away," I say. "But not too far."

There aren't any straws. I should have thought of straws when I bought the fruit. He takes a clean spoon from the drawer.

"It's good," he says. Only two spoonfulls. "But I'm not really hungry."

"How about you eat this much more?" I tap on his glass a quarter of the way down.

"I'll save it for later."

He means it. He thinks he'll eat it later, but he won't.

"Can I watch cartoons?" he says.

I put my hands on his shoulders and kiss the top of his head. A blessing I hide in affection. "Go ahead," I say. He walks into the living room and turns on the TV.

It's not that I expect the pills to make a difference. But I want to believe they will more than anything. I want to believe they can help him beyond what is reasonable to believe.

Our glasses are on the counter, still full. I taste mine. It's good but I'm not hungry either.

My son is right, it's not really a milkshake. It's called a licaudo. If we were in Cabo San Lucas there are carts all over town that sell them, and we would have one made for us every morning.

MTV Poem #17
Boyz II Men, *Motownphilly*

Daniel Romo

Start with the pelvic thrust. This shows that you're *not too hard, not too soft*. Careers begin by dreaming in high school, so teachers should encourage students to bypass classwork in favor of sleep. Nothing says success like synchronized dance steps from well-dressed, young black men. Changing outfits frequently is integral to a four-part harmony. Furthermore, never underestimate a man sporting the combination of a blazer, denim shorts, and a cane. Standing above an oversized birthday cake for no apparent reason is like standing above an oversized birthday cake for no apparent reason. But sitting outside the bathroom stall of a shitting man is the master plan to getting noticed. Sharing your spotlight with never-will-bes benefits no one. But the bond that East coast families share is thicker than all of the muck in the Atlantic. The neon from the sign in Geno's Steaks looks, simply, mouthwatering… Philadelphia is the City of Brotherly Love because everyone in the group is a lead singer. Nothing is more intimate than someone saying they're *kickin' it just for you.*

Harbinger

Kelly Jones

I left the light on and moths have swarmed.
Shooing them away as I step outside,
a few fly in but I don't worry.

They're moths, not the black widow I squished
in the corner or the bugs that eat our doorframes.

Sawdust piles up but they never show themselves.
I wish they would so I could Google how to kill them.

In the drizzle of half past midnight
I forget the moths while smoking.

In the drizzle of half past midnight it's nice out.
Quiet and still like a painting in a gallery downtown
where the tourists buy memories.

I come back in and dress for bed.
A moth flies into my closet and I wonder
what my clothes will look like in the morning.
Just how quickly can a wardrobe be ruined?

Repeater

Wendy C. Ortiz

We sit in the candlelight and I ignore the timid steps I hear scuffling then quieting in the grass. We have walked down to the secret café, Burt and I, and have joined others at a table. For what, I'm not sure. The table has a red and white checkered plastic cloth on it. I lay my oversized green sweater on the back of the folding chair and place my pack of Dunhill and a little white lighter on the table. *Ooh*, Burt says at the package of cigarettes. He likes shiny, noisy things and things that make smoke, and chemicals. I know he'll ask for one later.

Polka music plays from somewhere inside the house as two conversations run their parallel lines at our table. Telephone wires converge above the house, swaying in the light wind. I notice one woman I don't know, who is sitting at the next table over, pausing, listening in on Burt and I, which means I'm pausing to notice her, too, and I wait before answering whatever Burt's asked me.

The polka music blathers on rather riotously.

Jen arrives with the baby a quarter of an hour later. She sits down in a chair Burt pulls up beside his. The baby, Jen's first, though we don't know yet there will be others, later, jerks around on Jen's lap and I murmur his name, enjoying the sharp 's' and delicate 'k' sounds on my tongue, and I touch his tiny fingertips and the green felt of his homemade hat. The night requires no sweater, and soon the fireworks will begin. I wonder what the baby will make of the primary-colored explosions in the sky, the loud and staccato convulsions of his universe. I wonder many things about this baby, and about Jen, who has a tattoo on her ankle, the symbol for women, doubled. Jen passes the baby to Burt, who jiggles him, then steadies him, then dabs spittle from his tiny heart-like mouth. I figure my Dunhills will have to wait or relocate.

When the fireworks begin, conversations are halted. I want to say I hate fireworks but heads are turned and the polka music gets louder. I try to carry on my conversation with Burt, who passes the baby to me. I take the baby onto my lap and his squirmy attention turns to the glimmering, crackling sky. The light reflects on his face and his big baby eyes are round, mirror-like, and his mouth stays open like a little funnel. I rub his back and try to divert Burt's attention from the pyrotechnics, but finally I give up, letting the string of conversation fall somewhere between the horns and accordion and bass drums.

The polkas sound strangely familiar. I stare at the citronella candles standing guard around us and hold the baby whose head strains around whenever the colors in the sky stop momentarily, and I am wishing I was not at this table, wishing I could smoke a cigarette, be in the city, drinking a red wine with some new lover...until Burt reignites the conversation, turning towards Jen—and the baby strains to see Jen and begins to whimper. I contemplate for a second my breasts that don't have what the baby wants, and I am glad. Burt passes the baby back to Jen from my arms and finally, thankfully, asks me for a cigarette.

We smoke together at another table while Jen changes the baby. I watch her as we smoke and talk of Burt's latest business venture, and I wonder if Jen can instinctively feel whether the baby is in danger of suddenly rolling off her lap as she searches the bag for a clean cloth diaper. I smoke my cigarette to the end, knowing a headache is inevitable, but fine. The polka music suddenly seems appropriate, as well as the fireworks, and this baby at the next table over who does not belong to me. I consider that we might even be a scene in a semi-interesting movie; the candlelight, polka music, the fireworks—perhaps we're in a hamlet in an Eastern European country—I having never been to Europe—and when I put my cigarette out and acknowledge the pain reverberating in my skull, I wonder if we are the bit parts or main characters.

When the server, a comely pixie with a thrift store vintage apron around her waist, comes around and asks if we are sick of the music yet, we scoff at the suggestion.

Well, she explains, *it's an eight track and it's been playing the same three songs over and over.* She shrugs. *It's stuck.*

Ohhh, we all say. I knew it had sounded familiar. Like a film stuck on the reels as sometimes happened in the town's art house theater. Repeating, repeating.

The Dress Over Me

Kim Chinquee

"You're beautiful," I say to my aunt.

She tells me, "You're a knockout."

The salesladies keep bringing me more dresses: some in blue and red and orange, some aqua and some purple. I try them on, meeting up with my aunt in the three-way in the clothes of her own.

She says, "Does this look OK for a reunion?" She turns yet again.

"You look great," I say. I see then curves in her arms, her legs, her hips. I see rises in her cheekbones. As I watch her view herself, I feel skinny and old in the paisley bright dress that I liked on me until now.

I try on an orange-colored jumper. Then I try a black one. I step out, turning myself at different angles, sharing the mirror with my aunt. In her striped dress, I see some part of me, by the way she holds her gut in. She says, "I'm not usually like this."

The next year, a saleslady says, "That outfit really suits you."

Flowers in pink and blue form patterns on my chest.

I am trying on clothes in that same dressing room with one mirror and a curtain.

After my aunt's diagnosis, she left me lots of money. After losing her hair and breast, she got two separate DWIs which forced her into treatment. She ODed on pain meds.

Salesladies keep bringing me more clothes: long skirts and then short ones, crop pants and dresses so thin I can almost see through them.

The Urologist

Susannah Breslin

The urologist positioned himself so that he was standing between the wife, who was sitting in a chair with her back against the wall, and the husband, who was lying on the examination table with his pants around his ankles. The urologist massaged the husband's nut sack and gazed into the distance. The husband turned his head, pretending it wasn't happening. The husband's nuts were crooked; this was the problem.

The first time the husband and the wife had sex—of course, this was before the husband was the husband and the wife was the wife—the wife had noticed the husband's right nut hung lower than his left nut. At the time, the wife hadn't said anything about it. What could she have said that would not have ruined the moment?

After they were married, the wife had little reason to look at the husband's nut sack. The husband was a silverback gorilla. He climbed atop her in the dark of the night, inserted himself inside her, and did his business. The wife preferred this: no clambering foreplay, no probing tongue, no dithering about. The husband was nothing if not efficient.

Recently, though, the husband had returned from a business trip, his nut sack swollen. Not swollen with desire. Troublingly swollen.

In the bedroom, the wife had sat on the edge of the bed and taken the husband's nut sack in her hand.

"See?" the husband had said.

"Yes," the wife had said. The wife had squeezed the husband's nut sack gently. She had been able to feel the testes inside the envelope of skin.

"I don't feel a lump," the husband had said, strangled.

"I don't either," the wife had said. The testes had slid around in the fluid. The wife had made sure to keep her face a calm sea. Supposedly, the husband was the strong one. She knew better.

Several years ago, the wife had quit her job, making her financially dependent upon the husband. Which both of them preferred. Who needed independence, anyway? When you were married, autonomy was a ship sailing over a distant horizon.

The husband's nut sack had been warm in her hand—feral, unknowable, containing multitudes of unspent bullets.

"It's not cancer," the wife had announced. She wasn't an oncologist, but at her old job, she had a coworker who was black, and he had testicular cancer, and he had had a lump in his nut sack. This wasn't that.

"OK," the husband had said, sounding relieved, and stepped backwards, slipping himself out of her grasp.

"I know exactly what this is," the urologist murmured in the exam room, his gloved fingers fondling the husband's nut sack.

When the urologist had stepped into the room, he had been surprised to find the wife in the room with the husband. She wasn't going anywhere. The husband was as much her property as she was the husband's.

As far as she was concerned, marriage wasn't a life sentence; it was a death sentence. Marriage wasn't about two people living together; it was about two people dying together. They weren't married; they were conjoined.

That very morning, she had gotten on her knees before the toilet and scrubbed the husband's spattered fecal matter off the porcelain bowl. Nothing could tear them apart. They would have to haul her screaming and clawing off the husband before she would ever let him go.

"This is a safety bubble," the husband had told her not long after they were married. His face solemn, he had drawn a big circle around them in the air. She had understood what he was saying.

Sometimes, at dinner parties, someone would ask her why she had married the husband, and she would say, "If there is ever a zombie apocalypse, my husband will hunt other humans for us to eat." Invariably, the person would laugh, thinking she was joking, and she would laugh, too, playing along. She wasn't kidding. The husband was a killer.

The husband's face reflected in the mirror on the back of the exam room door was engaged in a battle over wanting to be worried and not wanting to show it.

"All right," the urologist said and dropped the husband's limp penis back onto his muscular thigh. The urologist peeled off his gloves as he strode to the other side of the room. The husband stood and pulled up his pants.

"It's not cancer," the urologist announced.

The wife made a low grunting noise no one heard, which was the sound of her letting go. There was an issue with the husband's nut sack—something mechanical. There would be minor surgery. It was no big deal. The nut sack would be restored.

The wife picked up her purse and hooked the strap over her shoulder. She wanted to grab the anatomical model of the male reproductive system sitting on the shelf next to her and smash it over the urologist's head. She had been that scared.

The husband had put on a different face, the one that said, I am the husband, and you are the wife, and everything is going to be fine.

She half-listened to what the urologist was telling the husband. She wondered how long she would have to wait before she could walk out the door. The husband had been to war twice, it had taken her decades to find him, and she was going to get her happy ending, for fuck's sake.

WHY TEACHERS GET FAT

MR. WOLF © ARONNEISSTEINKE.COM 1/2/2015

Counter

Vandoren Wheeler

> Throughout her six silent weeks,
> I stacked flimsy hope on top
> of hope, like an idiotic architect.

A Saturday morning,
I woke to dramatic knocking.
The courier "served" me
a white envelope fat
with court papers—

> I tried to dice onions
> instead of tear a hole
> in the floor and crawl
> under the false world.

For the first time, I imagined
her face pressed against
the word *bitch*—I smacked
the kitchen counter
as if squashing a wasp
I thought might lay
its evil eggs in me.

My palm throbbed with a pleasant,
self-righteous heat
I applied to my cheek

        as I chewed, slowly, the wasp,
        to let its venom numb
        the new tongue strange in my mouth.

The Escape Artists

Matt Bell

I.

Under allegations that it had been the sisters' songs that drew in their suitors, the younger and the older came to be called "the sirens"—but it was only the sisters who were dashed upon the rocks.

Because it had been their appearance that inspired the suitors' offenses, they were named for some time "the muses"—but the sisters' own poems grew empty of feeling, as if something had been taken that could not be taken back.

When they were pursued into the heart of the forest, they became trees themselves, barked and branched, laurels, "the frustrations." And even this protection from the gods did not stop other suitors from leaving their mark, from carving their names into their skin.

After they were chased off the high casts of the cliffs, they became "the echoes," impossible to capture, soon to fade. And only one among the suitors remembered their voices, a boy younger than all the rest, who had chased only because the others did; who had chased from the back of the pack, with no hope of being the one who caught them; who despite that lack had truly wanted them both, before and after their voices' long fall.

When the sisters retreated into the high and impenetrable keep to prevent the suitors from following, the suitors spread rumors that both the younger and the older had become "as beasts," shut away for their great ugliness. The tale spread to other villages, of the two girls covered in fur, sprouting horn and fang, and if the sisters never heard the tales themselves they did not mind the result, a life full of dancing objects and magical feasts, where there were no men to interrupt their reverie.

When the sisters came to prefer their chores for their own sake, the angry suitors begged the gods to punish them, for refusing to bring their talents into the house of their would-be husbands. What god was it then, who turned the older into a spider, so that she might weave forever, and which was it that turned the younger into a mouse, so that she might at last find every last crumb upon the kitchen floor? The sisters came to be called "the domestics," and it was their punishment the village women judged the harshest.

II.

The younger could not speak the words to say what the father had done, so she climbed the tallest tree in the woods behind the house, and, when she at last reached its top, she leapt out, fell down.

After her face was ruined the older could not forget how beautiful she had been, so one morning she lay down in the sand at the edge of the beach, making the decision to drown one inch at a time, beneath a caress of rising tide.

After her lover ended his shame by falling upon his sword, then on the anniversary of his death the younger took her own life with its inherited edge, its steel still somehow warm with the spectacle of his loss.

Cringing at the unseemliness of hanging, the older preferred to throw herself each time from the city walls, where her remains were no less public, but at least left in the fashion of her choosing.

Because they burned all of her paintings—because they broke her palettes and tore the bristles from her brushes—the older poured all her many paints out into the clawfoot bathtub, and when their thick pigments clogged the drain, then she climbed in and painted herself what, after the mixing of her thrashing, seemed a single glossy color.

Because she had swallowed so many poisoned apples, the townspeople made the older a coffin of lead, so that the remainder of her sadness would not pollute the ground.

You can tell the story again and again but the tragedy of this story is that you can change every detail but the last, what they did to themselves; and the first, what was done to them without their consent.

Unable to remove the unfair blame placed upon her, the best of all the youngers burned herself in a great fire. Afterward the townspeople made her a coffin of gold, so that her remains would shine just as brightly, for all the time her example was displayed, or else they donated their jewels, so that her otherwise plain coffin might shine as she once had. Or else because they did not know where to put her, they put her in the ground. Or else they put her on a mountaintop.

Or else they gave her to a dragon, a troll, a band of ogres. Or else they hung her from a tree. Or else they surrounded her with candles, flowers, attendant ladies-in-waiting. There were so many ways to say they were sorry that it was impossible to choose. There were so many places in which to do penance, to pray, and by the time they affixed the gold plate bearing her name to her casket, by then the whole of their world was praying silent as if in a church.

Two Fish

Tom Saya

(1)
There are two fish in this poem,
a red one and a green one.

I have seen them making ripples
on the surface, feeding on the insects
born of these words which
float, seemingly, without intention.

It's an entire eco-system, really,
complete with tree swallows
skimming a reflected sky.

Now that I have created this, I must
tend to it, see it to some conclusion.

It is of these fish that I need more
than just an occasional glimpse;
I need to hold them, distort
their mass in my hands,
take their underwater breaths,

though my shadow always warns them,
no matter how I trick my lines.

Now that I have created this, I
can't abandon it; I can only make
more paths and hope that one of them
will at least begin in the right place.

There's a faint scent of orchid, but
the undergrowth is humid and thick.
I'm afraid to step off of these stanzas,
like in quicksand, to who knows what depth.

I throw out more words, and the fish
come to them, but the sun is setting,
and the mosquitos are starting to bite.

You would think nothing could be
as innocuous as writing a poem.

(2)
There are two fish in this poem,
a red one and a green one.

I don't want them here;
this poem was not to have to
do with aquatic life, rivers,
lakes, or water in general.

Yet, it is sopping wet
and starting to rain.

The fish look at me
awaiting instructions or purpose.

You would think nothing could be
as selfish as writing a poem.

(3)
There are two fish in this poem,
a red one and a green one.

The red and green are not symbolic,
just colors, as everything is colored.

The two fish are here because
they are written in the above line,

though it is a bit curious how
they keep swimming down this poem

as though it were a river
that would take them to an ocean.

How slippery metaphor is, insinuating
itself here against my intention.

This is just supposed to be a portrait,
a celebration of the red and green fish.

It is just trying to see them as
they are: their glass-like gills

and shimmery sun-lit iridescence as
seen through the trick of water.

In the next draft of this poem
I must get rid of "glass," and

I'll have to describe the fish more.
The more I think about it

this poem just isn't working
so I'll scrap the whole thing,

but first I'll write them their ocean.
You would think nothing could be

as unreal as writing a poem.

(4)
There are two fish in this poem,
a red one and a green one.

I dive in and follow them down,
down until I can barely see them,
down until we finally start to climb,
and climb until we reach the surface
of the other side of this poem,
sort of like digging to China,
but I'm still in this chair, this room,
only everything is backwards. I'm
uncomfortable; things are not right.

I dive back in but cannot find the way back.

If I look in a mirror things are
right, but, of course, they aren't:
reflections only get me back to where I was.

Shipwrecked, I gather what might be
useful from the hold and head inland
from the shores of this poem.

Contributors

Rafael Alvarez came of age on the City Desk of the *Baltimore Sun* across the final chapters of the once-celebrated paper's influence and greatness. There, he befriended all manner of characters—dishwashers and detectives and dance hall queens—who would find their way into his fiction. A writer for the first three seasons of the HBO drama *The Wire*, Alvarez published a new collection of short stories in 2014, *Tales from the Holy Land*. He can be reached via orlo.leini@gmail.com.

Matt Bell is the author of the novel *In the House upon the Dirt between the Lake and the Woods*, a finalist for the Young Lions Fiction Award, a Michigan Notable Book, an Indies Choice Adult Debut Book of the Year Honor Recipient, and the winner of the Paula Anderson Book Award. His next novel, *Scrapper*, will be published in Fall 2015. He teaches creative writing at Arizona State University.

Susannah Breslin is the author of *You're a Bad Man, Aren't You?*

S. Cearley's work has been featured in *Floating Bridge Review (#7)*, *Lockjaw Magazine*, and *Entropy*.

Kim Chinquee is the author of the collections *Pretty, Pistol* and *Oh Baby*. Her work has appeared in *The Nation, Huffington Post, Noon, Conjunction, Ploughshares, Storyquarterly, The Pushcart Prize, Denver Quarterly*, and several other journals and anthologies. Her website is www.kimchinquee.com.

Susan DeFreitas is a writer, editor, educator, and spoken word artist. Her work has appeared in *The Utne Reader*, *The Nervous Breakdown*, *Southwestern American Literature*, *Fourth River*, *Weber—The Contemporary West*, and *Bayou Magazine*, among other publications. She is the author of the fiction chapbook *Pyrophitic* (ELJ Publications, 2014), and holds an MFA from Pacific University. Susan lives in Portland, Oregon, where she serves as an associate editor with Indigo Editing & Publications and a reader for *Tin House Magazine*.

Steve Denniston lives in SE Portland, Oregon. His most recent publications include a story with the *Work Literary Magazine* in October and a story in Forest Avenue Press's anthology, *The Night, The Rain, and The River*.

JJ Chen Henderson, M.D., Ph. D., writes fiction and poetry. Her works appear in *Poetry East*, *Fourteen Hills*, *LUMINA*, *The Comstock Review*, *Concho River*, *ELJ Publications*, *TSR Publishing*, and *SLANT*, among others. JJ lives in a windy town in West Texas with her husband and their eleven-year-old daughter, Kate.

Shane Hinton holds an MFA from the University of Tampa and lives in the winter strawberry capital of the world. His debut story collection *Pinkies* will be available June 16, 2015 from Burrow Press.

Lily Hoang is the author of four books, including *Changing*, recipient of a PEN Open Books Award. With Joshua Marie Wilkinson, she edited the anthology *The Force of What's Possible: Writers on the Avant-Garde and Accessibility*. She teaches in the MFA program at New Mexico State University, where she is Associate Department

Head. She serves as Prose Editor at *Puerto del Sol* and Creative Non-Fiction Editor at *Drunken Boat*.

William Jolliff serves as professor of English at George Fox University. Bill has published critical articles and poems in over a hundred periodicals, including *Northwest Review*, *Southern Humanities Review*, *Midwest Quarterly*, *Christianity and Literature*, and *Appalachian Journal*. His new book, *Twisted Shapes of Light*, is forthcoming from Cascade Press.

Kelly Jones works and plays in New Orleans. A good deal of her adult life has been devoted to obtaining pieces of paper that verify her knowledge of things (resulting in an MFA in Poetry and a BA in Literature and Social Justice). She is terribly fond of manatees, glitter, Wild Turkey, and dance parties. In her spare time she runs *The Gambler Mag*, lazes by the bayou, and tries to come to terms with the concept of infinity.

Dana Koster was a Wallace Stegner Fellow and a 2012 recipient of the Dorothy Sargent Rosenberg Prize. Her poems have appeared or are forthcoming in *Indiana Review*, *Southern Humanities Review*, *The Cincinnati Review*, *PN Review*, and *EPOCH*, among others. She lives in California's Central Valley with her husband and young son.

Michael Mejia is the author of the novel *Forgetfulness* and his fiction and nonfiction have appeared in many journals and anthologies, including *Agni*, *Diagram*, *Seneca Review*, and *My Mother She Killed Me, My Father He Ate Me*. He has received a Literature Fellowship in Prose from the NEA and a grant from the Ludwig Vogelstein Foundation. Editor-in-chief of *Western Humanities Review* and co-founding editor of Ninebark Press, he teaches creative writing at the University of Utah.

Lydia Netzer is the author of *Shine Shine Shine*, a New York Times Notable Book and finalist for the LA Times Book Prize. Her most recent novel is *How to Tell Toledo From the Night Sky*. She lives in Virginia with her husband, children, dogs, and horse.

Wendy C. Ortiz is the author of *Excavation: A Memoir and Hollywood Notebook*. Her work has appeared in *The New York Times*, *McSweeney's Internet Tendency, Vol. 1 Brooklyn*, *The Rumpus*, and *Brain, Child*, among many other journals. Wendy is a marriage and family therapist intern in Los Angeles. Visit www.wendyortiz.com.

Joanna Lynne Ponce is a transgender, Mexican-American writer living in Portland, Oregon. She earned an undergraduate degree at San Francisco State University and a graduate degree at Oregon State University. Her fiction writing, while largely unpublished, focuses on the themes of personal identity, family, love, loss, and triumph. She credits her love of story to her Mexican grandparents and ancestry. These days she is enjoying her retirement by exploring the beauty and wonders of the Pacific Northwest.

Jay Ponteri has published one memoir and one chapbook. The memoir (*Wedlocked*, Hawthorne Books 2013) won the Oregon Book Award for Creative Nonfiction. The chapbook is titled *Darkmouth Strikes Again*, published by Future Tense Books. He has recently published nonfiction in *Essay Daily*, *Tinhouse.com*, *Ghost*

Proposal, and *Forklift, Ohio*. He is currently reading *Superior Packets: Three Books* by Susie Timmons (Wave Books). He lives in Portland.

Daniel Romo is the author of *When Kerosene's Involved* (Mojave River Press, 2014) and *Romancing Gravity* (Silver Birch Press, 2013). His writing can be found in *The Los Angeles Review, Gargoyle, MiPOesias*, and elsewhere. He is the Co-founder/Editor at *Wherewithal* and is the head Poetry Editor for *Cease, Cows*. He lives in Long Beach, CA and at danielromo.net.

In 2000, Clackamas Literary Review published two of **Lois Rosen's** poems. Most recently her writing has appeared in *Calyx, Alimentum, VoiceCatcher*, and the *Jewish Women's Literary Annual*. She's taught writing at Willamette University and ESL at Chemeketa Community College.

Kevin Sampsell is the author of the novel, *This Is Between Us* (Tin House) and the memoir, *A Common Pornography* (HarperCollins). His collage art has been featured in *Kolaj Magazine, Jerkpoet, Lazy Fascist Review, Ohio Edit, Queen Mobs Teahouse*, and in his collage column, *Paper Trumpets*, which appears on *The Rumpus*.

Tom Saya was educated at Indiana University and the University of North Carolina—Greensboro. He is currently teaching at Tennessee Technological University in Cookeville, TN. His work has appeared in *Poetry East, The South Carolina Review, Artful Dodge, The Midwest Quarterly*, and various other literary journals.

Katherine Clarke Sinback earned her MA in Writing from Portland State University. She publishes her zine *Crudbucket* and writes two blogs: the online companion to *Crudbucket*, and *Peabody Project Chronicles 2: Adventures in Pregnancy After Miscarriage*. Born and raised in Virginia, Katie lives in Portland, Oregon, with her family.

Noel Sloboda's poetry has recently appeared in *Pank*, *Rattle*, *Harpur Palate*, *Salamander*, *Redactions*, and *Weave*. He is the author of the poetry collections *Shell Games* (Sunnyoutside, 2008) and *Our Rarer Monsters* (Sunnyoutside, 2013) as well as several chapbooks. Sloboda has also published a book about Edith Wharton and Gertrude Stein. He teaches at Penn State York.

Ben Slotky is the author of *Red Hot Dogs, White Gravy*, and *An Evening of Romantic Lovemaking*. His work has appeared in *The Santa Monica Review*, *McSweeneys*, *Golden Handcuffs Review*, and other journals. He lives in Bloomington, IL.

Aron Nels Steinke lives in Portland, Oregon, with his wife and son. Aron is a second grade teacher by day and cartoonist by night. His latest children's book, *The Zoo Box*, was a collaboration with his wife, Ariel Cohn. Steinke describes it as an early reader thriller where two siblings discover a zoo in which human and animal roles are reversed.

Rosalynn Stovall is a writer and video artist. She recently received her MFA in visual art from the Sam Fox School of Design & Visual Arts. Her writing has previously appeared in *Monkey Bicycle*, *Flash: The International Short-Short Story Magazine*, and *Number: An Inde-*

pendent Journal of the Arts. She currently lives in St. Louis, MO, with her husband and infant daughter.

Nick Triolo is a writer, activist, filmmaker, photographer, and runner currently living in Missoula, Montana, where he is pursuing a graduate degree at the University of Montana. He is Senior Editor of Camas *Environmental Literary Magazine* <www.camasmagazine.org>, and his work has been published in *Trail Runner Magazine*, *Camas Magazine*, *Terrain.org* (forthcoming—end of November), *Ultrarunner Magazine*, *iRunfar*, *Territory Run Co*, and *Patagonia's Dirtbag Diaries Podcast*. See more of his work at *The Jasmine Dialogues*. <jasminedialogues. wordpress.com>

Vandoren Wheeler was born in Las Cruces, New Mexico. He cracked his head open on the playground in various ways in the 2nd, 4th, and 6th grades; he began writing seriously in the 8th grade. He has published poems in fine publications such as *H_ngM_n*, *Forklift*, *Swink*, and *ratemyprofessors.com*. His manuscript *The Accidentalist* won the Dorothy Brunsman Prize and was published by Bear Star Press in late 2012. He currently teaches in Portland, Oregon, and is tweaking his manuscript *Lonely & Co.*

Robert Wrigley is Distinguished University Professor of English at the University of Idaho. His most recent books include *Anatomy of Melancholy & Other Poems* (Penguin, 2013), and, in the United Kingdom, *The Church of Omnivorous Light: Selected Poems* (Bloodaxe Books, 2013). He lives in the woods with his wife, the writer Kim Barnes.

Born in Puerto Rico, **John Yohe** grew up in Michigan and currently lives in Portland, Oregon. He has worked as a wildland firefighter, deckhand/oiler, runner/busboy, bike messenger, wilderness ranger, and fire lookout, as well as a teacher of writing. A complete list of his publications, and poetry, fiction and non-fiction writing samples, can be found at his website: www.johnyohe.com

Visit

clackamasliteraryreview.org
facebook.com/clackamasliteraryreview

Contact
clr@clackamas.edu

CLACKAMAS LITERARY REVIEW

the finest writing for the best readers

Clackamas Literary Review has been committed to bringing you the best writing from around the world since 1997. Subscribe now to receive the latest and forthcoming issues.

Clackamas Literary Review

_____	1 year	$10
_____	2 years	$18
_____	3 years	$26

Name _____

Address _____

City / State / Zip _____

Email _____

Send this form and check or money order to:

Clackamas Literary Review
English Department
Clackamas Community College
19600 Molalla Avenue
Oregon City, Oregon 97045

CPSIA information can be obtained at www.ICGtesting.com
Printed in the USA
BVOW11s1349030415

394177BV00008B/12/P